Awakening Minds

Awakening Minds

The Power of Creativity in Teaching

James Downton, Jr.

Humanics Trade Group
Atlanta, GA USA

HUMANICS

Awakening Minds
A Humanics Trade Group Publication
First Edition

© 2003 by Brumby Holdings, Inc.

Humanics trade Group Publications are an imprint of and published by Humanics Publishing Group, a division of Brumby Holdings, Inc. Its trademark, consisting of the words "Humanics Trade Group" and a portrayal of a Pegasus, is registered in the U.S. Patent Office and in other countries.

Brumby Holdings, Inc.
1197 Peachtree St.
Suite 533B Plaza
Atlanta, GA 30361
USA

Printed in the United States of America and the United Kingdom

Library of Congress Control Number: 2002112064
ISBN (Paperback): 0-89334-360-9
ISBN (Hardcover): 0-89334-361-7

Dedication

*For the teachers
who responded to my invitation
to become more creative.*

*I will always remember
your changes,
sense of adventure,
and courage.*

*Your positive impact on
the education and
lives of students
is inspiring.*

Creative Spirit:
"You're going on a trip.
No need to pack your bags,
just unpack your mind.
Make room for new ideas."

Contents

Chapter 5: Engage Students In Active Learning 29

"Tell me and I'll forget. Show me and I'll learn. Involve me and I'll understand." Students become involved when we create experiential exercises that awaken and engage their minds. By emphasizing active learning, we see a sudden rise in students' attention and receptivity.

Chapter 6: Be Willing To Take Risks 35

Fear permeates education. Teachers and students alike may hold back for fear of being wrong or looking foolish. Those fears add too much caution to learning. We discover how to reduce the size of our fears in order to bring new vitality to teaching and education.

Chapter 7: Manage The Size Of Your Ego 43

Ego is concern for oneself and its survival. The smaller the ego feels, the more it tries to inflate its size. Education is dramatically affected by teachers and students trying to manage the size of their egos. We use "Recovery Claims" to keep our egos from shrinking.

Chapter 8: Create Motivation And Participation . . .53

Motivation and participation can be created. We learn to motivate our students by designing learning exercises on "the four cornerstones of motivation." We increase their participation by understanding what holds them back.

Chapter 9: Community Service Stimulates Learning . . .61

When students serve in the community while learning in the classroom, their motivation escalates. With greater interest, their engagement with issues deepens, so classroom learning becomes more dynamic.

Chapter 10: Cultivate Inspiration 65

The mind becomes more playful when it is surprised. One way to surprise it is by creating arbitrary "inspiration points." This adds a steady stream of novelty to teaching. By learning to create our own inspiration, we discover how easy it is to generate ideas for teaching.

Chapter 11: Develop Novel Ideas For Teaching 71

It is easy to fall into a rut while teaching. To discover new ideas and approaches, we travel down unusual pathways. We use "Object Play" and "Mind Switching" to stimulate our search. When we do, we find creative ideas coming to us with little effort. Fun is added to teaching.

Teachers invent stories about students. When the stories are negative, relationships with students suffer. When they are positive, good relationships develop. By revising our stories, we nurture more positive relationships with our students. This increases mutual trust and respect.

We can become so overworked as teachers, we fall out of balance, feel miserable, and lose our enthusiasm for teaching. Recovering balance helps us to create a greater sense of contentment. While innovating, we accommodate conflicting inner voices, then balance workloads.

We may live in stories of belief that limit us and make us miserable as teachers. Assumptions are beliefs that limit our thinking. Ideals are beliefs that can lead to disappointment and unhappiness. We change our stories so teaching becomes more creative and enjoyable.

Resisting what cannot be changed produces frustration. Becoming resigned to situations that can be changed causes alienation When we give up resistance and resignation, we create a new sense of freedom and greater ease in teaching.

Teachers often ask questions without a clear sense for their impact on the activity of the mind. Questions guide what the mind thinks about and how deeply it engages an issue. We learn to use questions consciously to deepen inquiry, expand options, and empower students to change.

Listening usually occurs on the surface. Facts and feelings may be heard, but needs and desires for change are often missed. By learning to listen at four levels, we hear more as teachers, which gives us the ability to deepen any discussion and to solve problems more effectively.

Chapter 18: Leading Dynamic Discussions 119
Discussions are great learning opportunities when they are focused and dynamic. When we listen deeply and ask probing questions, we engage the interest of students and intensify their learning. The ability to lead dynamic discussions gives our teaching greater impact.

Chapter 19: Be Receptive To Coaching 129
When receiving "criticism," a teacher's ego is likely to deflate, so listening stops. "Defend" and "counterattack" may be automatic. We discover how we respond to criticisms, then develop greater receptivity to coaching and change. Our effectiveness increases as a result.

Chapter 20: Coach Effectively 137
When teachers give feedback to students, it is often negative. Using the "Sandwich Technique" while coaching, we create a better balance between positive and negative feedback. We show students what they are doing well and what they might change.

Chapter 21: "Nightmare" Students 145
"Nightmare" students present unique and creative challenges. There are the "unmotivated," "critics," "minimalists," and "tormentors." Like sleeping nightmares, we wish they did not exist, but they do. How we teach can also make normal students into nightmares.

Chapter 22: Creativity Is Always Possible 151
When circumstances seem too limiting, we may play it safe and take a conventional approach rather than be creative. Imposed requirements or teaching a large class may weaken our resolve to the point where we forget that using a creative approach is always possible.

Chapter 23: Teaching Wisdom 167
"Wisdom" is not a word often heard in teaching. Yet, when we ask questions about wisdom, the mind gladly seeks answers. We discover the power of wisdom to open new understandings about any issue. We use wisdom as a crucial part of our creativity as teachers.

Creative teaching enlivens education, deepens a teacher's impact on the thinking and lives of students, and leads to a sense of greater fulfillment. Imagining those possibilities for ourselves, we discover why we became teachers.

Appreciation

*F*or more than twenty-five years, I have been encouraging teachers to expand their creativity through experiential workshops. At intervals, I also teach a graduate seminar on creative teaching within my department. The graduate teachers in my seminar were a source of inspiration and help as I developed my ideas for this book. They created some of the sayings of the "creative spirit" that you will read throughout. I am grateful for their inspiration and contribution.

I want to thank my wife, Mary, who edited my writing to make it clear and easy to read.

There are many forms of creativity. Some are pursued by people in organizations who see a vision of a better future for others and commit their lives to it. One such organization is "I Have A Dream" Foundation. It mentors and inspires children from low-income families to attend and graduate from college. The children (called "Dreamers") receive a financial scholarship upon completion of their college degrees. Many local chapters of the foundation raise funds for this purpose. Through their encouragement and support, many children who would never have considered attending college have graduated or are college students today. Half of my royalties from *Awakening Minds* will go to this worthwhile and effective organization. To learn more about the nature of its work, see page 179 at the back of this book and visit its website [www.ihad.org].

Becoming A More Creative Teacher

$\mathcal{J}$ completed my Ph.D. at the University of California at Berkeley, where my only exposure to teaching methods was the lecture style. Each day I watched my teachers walk to their lecterns, take out their pages of notes, and launch into their lectures. Many were so dependent on their notes that they seldom moved more than a few paces away from them. When I began teaching at San Francisco State University in 1965, I naturally adopted the same format. I prepared carefully crafted notes, gave my lectures, and engaged students in discussions of the issues. My effectiveness as a lecturer was reflected in the enthusiasm students expressed about my courses. This success reinforced my highly conventional approach to teaching. It was the honesty and good will of a student that led me to develop a more creative approach.

One semester, a bright young man enrolled in one of my classes. His papers were among the best and his contributions during discussions were always impressive. At the end of the term, he came up to me, shook my hand, and said: "Thank you, you're a very interesting book."

This was a rare moment of awakening for me. With my lecture style, I had become just another interesting book. I was perceptive enough to hear this young man's advice to alter my approach. I realized that I assigned interesting books for a course so I did not have to be a book myself.

On that day, I vowed to become a different kind of teacher. I would stop relying exclusively on lectures and would vary my teaching strategies to produce greater diversity in my approach. To engage the minds of my students so they were motivated to think, understand, and retain, I began emphasizing experiential learning combined with discussion. I included "mini-lectures" within the experiential teaching in order to integrate important theoretical ideas and information. Combining those approaches produced a dramatic rise in my students' participation, their receptivity to new information and ideas, and their motivation to learn. Whatever method I used, my commitment was to innovation. "How can I teach this topic in a creative way?" became a guiding question.

Creative Spirit:
"Remember the amazement and wonder
you felt the first time you explored a tide pool.
Instead of filling up your students with information,
engage them in the excitement of discovery."

As teachers, declaring our intention to be creative dramatically increases our ability to arouse the minds of our students so they can learn. What approach to creativity can help us get started?

Jerry Hirshberg, in *The Creative Priority*, gives us some starting points:

*"Creativity is the mastery of information
and skills in the service of dreams."*

*"Creativity does not play by the rules,
it plays with the rules."*

Hirschberg calls creativity "effective surprise," so whom must we surprise first? Ourselves of course.

"Creativity" is the capacity to think and behave in unconventional ways. This includes the cultivation of a more "playful mind," the part of us that thrives on flexibility, surprises, imagination, and risk-taking. A playful mind welcomes the opportunity to develop new ideas and novel approaches to issues. Its innovative efforts are aligned with the four little principles of learning and change.

Do,
Get feedback through "mistakes,"
Learn from the feedback,
Then change what you are doing.

Instead of fearing mistakes, the person who cultivates creativity appreciates and learns from them. When we are afraid of failure, our willingness to take risks diminishes, which undermines our capacity to teach with the full range of our creative powers. Becoming a more creative teacher requires continual experimentation, a willingness to take risks, and the capacity to embrace mistakes as helpful feedback to change what we are doing. When creative teaching is established as a goal, the chance of enlivening any aspect of education dramatically increases. When we develop our creative powers, teaching becomes an adventure that never stops. It is the closest thing to space travel in education.

I invite you into that adventure with this book. Being experiential, it takes you through exercises that will rely on your natural creativity in order to transform who you are as a teacher and to deepen your commitment to more innovative teaching as a calling. When creativity is more fully developed within you, you will feel more adventuresome, less afraid to try new approaches, and more excited to teach. As your students watch you being creative, they will come to value the importance of cultivating creativity in themselves.

Creative Spirit:
"You are Commander of the Starship Enterprise.
Your students are the crew.
What is your 'prime directive?'
To boldly go where no person has gone before."

What are the ultimate goals of elevating the creative spirit in education? Imagine an educational program which is deeply committed to nourishing greater creativity among teachers and students. Learning would become much more dynamic and exciting. Students would want to be engaged in thinking about important issues and would retain more of what they learned. Encouraged to be creative, their capacity to think in novel ways would expand. By emphasizing creativity, the way students learn would be infused with the excitement of discovery, so the spirit of education would be lifted up. More fully captivated by learning, students would become lifelong learners.

In preparation for the experiential work ahead, buy a large journal where you will complete the processes, maintain a record of your ideas, and design learning exercises for your classes. Consider giving your journal a title that establishes your commitment to be a more creative teacher. As you work through the experiential processes, take the opportunity to experiment with new ideas and different ways of teaching in your classes. Develop a new way to teach that inspires you, not just your students.

Creative Spirit:
"Old paths are comfortable, but may lack adventure.
New ones may be uncomfortable, but more exciting.
Which path do you choose?"

The book can be used in different ways. The greatest impact will achieved by doing the exercises from cover to cover, but you will also receive value by selecting chapters that are the most compelling for you. You can skip around the book, if that works best. Whatever approach you take, it is important not to read through the chapter before doing the learning processes in it. It takes the element of surprise out of the work, which weakens its impact.

The book is organized so you can do the work on your own, with another teacher, or a group of teachers. If you are working alone, you will need to find a partner for Chapters 17 and 20. I have included rough time estimates for each exercise, but they will be greater if you work with a partner or group because of the sharing that occurs. Working with a partner or group is especially rewarding, because the discussions of teaching will cultivate new ideas and you will receive support for innovation. Participating with a group of teachers provides an opportunity to teach the work by rotating who takes the leading role. Before guiding people through a chapter, do the learning processes on your own. You will discover special group processes in some chapters that you will enjoy doing together.

Some of the work you will do in *Awakening Minds* is drawn from ideas in two of my other books in The Life Gardening Project, *The Woo Way: A New Way of Living and Being* and *Playful Mind: Bringing Creativity To Life*. Those books include many learning exercises that you can use in your teaching to enhance the personal growth and creativity of your students. To explore their contents on the web, visit [http://lifegardening.com].

I welcome you into this work with a promise. If you do the exercises, you will expand your creativity and effectiveness as a teacher. You will see improvements in your ability to motivate your students to learn. As they become more deeply engaged in learning, you will see them grow in knowledge, ability, and effectiveness. As they grow, so will your enthusiasm for teaching. The following poem reflects those possibilities.

> *The creativity flowed*
> *in steady streams*
> *and sometimes*
> *in uncontrollable*
> *and enchanting gushes.*
> *Almost as if by magic,*
> *new forms of life*
> *could be seen*
> *growing everywhere.*

Chapter 1

Teaching With Purpose

"What are your life purposes and how are they related to your teaching?" Many teachers are caught off guard by this question, because they have never thought carefully about their life purposes, let alone how they bear on teaching. When teaching flows from meaningful life purposes, it becomes soul work, not just paid work. This soulful aspect of teaching is emphasized in Parker Palmer's *The Courage to Teach*, where he encourages teachers to discover and express their own uniqueness and passion. This is an alternative to simply emulating the styles of teachers we admire.

The direction and goals of teaching become more apparent when our life purposes are known. One teacher may aspire to cultivate tolerance and community. Another may want to unravel the mystery of "black holes." Consciously declaring our life purposes directly influences our teaching mission. Knowing our purposes and declaring our teaching mission puts a teaching road map in our hands.

Creative Spirit:
*"If you don't know where you're going,
you won't get there.
If you don't know why you're going there,
what's the point of making the trip?"*

Individual Process (20 minutes): In the middle of a journal page, write "My life purposes." Around the page scatter the various purposes you want your life to serve.

Add a purpose you have not allowed yourself to imagine.

Include a surprising possibility.

Circle your four most compelling purposes. Next to each one, jot down an idea about how it could be more fully realized through teaching.

Examining your life purposes, write a simple statement capturing your teaching mission. For example, my life purposes are to help people reduce their suffering, to enhance their well-being, to increase their creativity, and to do all those things for myself. My teaching mission is to "Help cultivate the development of human beings," which includes me. What is your mission? Make your statement simple, so you can easily recall it.

Take a few minutes to contemplate your purposes and mission, considering how they might shape a new orientation to teaching.

Briefly note some of the changes you will try.

If you are working with a partner or group, share what you discovered and created.

Creative Spirit:
"It's not that the lunch you offered wasn't good.
It's just the same old lunch.
Think about changing your lunch menu
by adding a few tempting entrees to your teaching."

Be Clear About Your Commitments

Knowing our life purposes and teaching mission helps to clarify our goals as teachers. Commitment is the conscious decision to reach those goals. If we find ourselves drifting from semester to semester without any direction, developing clear commitments will help us chart a definite course.

Individual Process (10 minutes): Divide a journal page in half.

On one half, note the goals you are committed to achieve for your students.

On the other half, note the goals you are committed to achieve in your development as a teacher.

Take one of your commitments and briefly describe how you will reach your goal.

If you are working with a partner or group share your discoveries.

When teaching encompasses life purposes, a clear mission, and conscious commitments, it becomes a more compelling part of our lives. On the days when the inevitable disappointments occur, our negative mood is acknowledged, then momentum is fully restored because of the deeper meaning teaching holds for us. Over time, it becomes inseparable from our identity. When that occurs, teaching changes from being a job into a calling. Then, we teach because we are compelled to.

Chapter 2

Identity Affects How You Teach

*H*umans are story tellers. We tell stories about everything –ourselves, teaching, students and our life circumstances. Our stories are composed of beliefs about what we think is true. Some of those beliefs shape the identity stories we tell about ourselves as teachers. When we question the beliefs that make up our stories, remodeling our identities becomes possible. Change our identity and new pathways in teaching quickly open up.

Creative Spirit:
*"What if you taught as if you were
a book of science fiction?
An intriguing novel? A gripping mystery?
A comic book?"*

Individual Process (30 minutes): Tear up a piece of paper into small parts. On each piece, write a quality you possess that influences your teaching. For example, you may be "well-informed" or "a hard worker." You may be "good with words" or have a "special talent to inspire students." Include negative qualities if they describe you. "Too controlling" or "overly sensitive" could be honest descriptions. What you regard as your qualities are the beliefs you hold about yourself as a teacher. Together, they make up your identity story.

When your qualities are noted, arrange them in the shape of a triangle, with your most important attribute at the top. The next two most important qualities would fall on the second line, with the left side of the triangle having the greater influence. Move your qualities around until the pattern clearly captures the identity story that you tell about yourself as a teacher.

Contemplate the pattern of your identity for a moment. Notice whether you have included "creative."

If you have, consider how the belief "I'm creative" affects how you feel about yourself as a person and what you undertake in teaching. If "creative" was in the triangle but not at the top, place it alongside your leading quality to shift the focus of your identity. If you want, put "creative" alone at the top to discover what happens.

If "creative" was not included, think about why and whether you would like it to be. If you would, then add "creative" to your identity. Out of curiosity, put it at the top alongside your leading attribute. If you find yourself saying "But I'm not creative," remember that identity is something you created over time by the choices you made. Since you created your identity, you can add to or subtract from it. It is like editing a story.

With "creative" at the top, examine the rest of your attributes. Move qualities that would support your creativity toward the top to strengthen it. For example, an attribute like "persistent" might be moved up. If you want, you can remove qualities that undermine your creativity.

Finally, on separate slips, record a few new qualities that would strengthen your identity as a more creative teacher. "Courageous" comes to mind. Place those qualities within the triangle where they would strengthen your creativity.

As you contemplate your creative identity, imagine what changes you could make in your teaching. Note:

■ One new risk you will take.
■ One new teaching strategy you will try.
■ One change that will alter your attitude toward teaching.

Sharper Focus: What is the most important issue about identity that has been raised for you? Relax into a few minutes of quiet reflection about it.

If you are working with a partner or group, share what you learned.

Creative Spirit:
"Boldly declaring that you're a creative teacher greatly improves your chances of becoming one."

When I guide teachers through this exercise in workshops, there are usually a few who cannot think of themselves as creative. I tell them that they can produce a similar result if they make a strong commitment to be creative. The commitment will bring creativity into existence almost as effectively as when it comes from identity. In either case, the persistent question in teaching becomes "What creative approach can I take here?" As soon as the question is raised, the mind will begin to develop innovative options.

As teachers, we cannot help creating identity stories that shape what we think and do. If those stories are too serious and narrow, creative thinking may suffer from the restrictions we impose on it. When our identities are more flexible and playful, the mind's ability to experiment and innovate expands. A more balanced identity might honor the idea of "serious play," where the weight of issues is recognized while the lighter spirit of creativity is also appreciated. "To give a fair chance to potential creativity is a matter of life and death for society," according to Arnold Toynbee. How can we be part of the teaching vanguard that gives creativity a chance?

Selling Images

A significant part of human communication is sales work. In teaching, we package ideas, theories, and values for the educational market place. As teachers, many of us also work hard to sell ourselves. What beliefs do we want our students, colleagues, and those higher in the status hierarchy to hold about us? What images are we packaging?

Individual Process (20 minutes): Divide a journal page in half. On one half, record beliefs you want students to hold about you. Those beliefs make up the image you want them to have of you as a teacher. Examining your work, convert it into an advertisement, as if you were the product being sold.

On the other half of the page, identify beliefs you want your colleagues and "higher-ups" to accept about you. What image do you want them to have of you? Write an advertisement, as if you were the product being sold.

Examine the two advertisements.

What do you notice?

How do the two images you are selling affect your creativity? What impact do they have on your enjoyment of teaching? Note at least two ways.

Removing any concern for how you will be perceived by others, write an advertisement of yourself that honestly reflects who you want to be as a teacher, where there is no interest at all in selling yourself. Give your advertisement a headline when it is finished.

What new opportunities emerge in your teaching when you stop trying to sell an image? Note at least two ideas.

If you are working with a partner or group, share your discoveries and any new choices.

Creative Spirit:
"What if you taught with a sign hanging from your neck inscribed with the words 'No image for sale'?"

When the sales work stops, freedom expands. When you have nothing to prove, you will nourish the part of you that loves to experiment and take risks. Instead of being stopped by your fears, you will welcome creativity for the refreshing sense of freedom, excitement, and pleasure it adds to teaching.

Chapter 3

Cultivate A More Playful Mind

$\mathcal{M}$ost of us have forgotten that we were taught to think within limits. In some ways, we are like trained falcons. To train a falcon, a long, leather tether is tied on its leg. The trainer holds the end of the tether securely in one hand as the bird is released to fly. When the falcon reaches the end of its tether, it recoils in shock. This is done many times, until it learns the limits of how far it can fly, then the tether is taken off. In the mind of the falcon, the tether is still tied to its leg, so flying away does not enter its thinking as a possibility. Its freedom is dramatically curtailed and it fails to notice it.

Instead of a tether, social norms and expectations have conditioned us to limit our ability to think creatively. Unaware of the imposed limits, we lost the possibility of greater freedom. While the falcon cannot become aware of how it was trained, we can. By understanding how we learned to conform, we declare the right to think outside of established limits. Becoming more creative as a teacher is an adventurous attempt to push beyond those boundaries.

When "serious" dominates teaching, it becomes like a tether on our thinking. It limits what we allow ourselves to think and say. As a consequence, teaching becomes measured and contained. By cultivating a more playful mind, thinking becomes more flexible and spontaneous, which nourishes the spirit of fun and an unending path of curiosity, experimentation, discovery, change, and renewal. To nourish more playful thinking, consider the "fun-da-mentals of creativity," where the "fun" always comes before the "mental."

Creative Spirit:
"Go to class with the intention of having fun.
See if you can walk out with a smile on your face."

The "Fun-da-mentals"

What leads us to contain our natural creativity are ego concerns about being accepted, looking good, being right, feeling secure, and being in control. Given those concerns, we learn to monitor our thinking, letting ideas through that seem socially respectable so people will accept rather than criticize us. Through that screening, playful mind is held back for fear of doing or saying something "wrong" or "stupid." The "fun-da-mentals of creativity" combat this tendency to be too restricted and careful. They help us get our egos out of the way, so our minds can play. This playfulness is what awakens the creative spirit in us as teachers.

■ Experience failures as feedback

Failures are feedback for the mind to change what it is doing. They are essential for learning.

■ Take risks

Risk is the adventurous cutting edge of creativity. If you are willing to take risks, new possibilities and talents will be cultivated. Risks stretch the mind and expand our learning potential. Instead of thinking of risk as dangerous, see it as your willingness to discover what is possible.

■ Be spontaneous

Allow the mind to be spontaneous. When ego concerns are held in check, thinking is freed.

■ Suspend judgment

Suspend judgment while creating new ideas. Premature judgment, such as "that's a ridiculous idea," stops the creative flow of the mind. Evaluate ideas later.

■ Use imagination

Imagination is the capacity to see what cannot yet be seen. Nothing loosens the rigidity of the mind more quickly.

Creative Spirit:
"While holding a rigid attitude,
see if you can get your mind to play."

Escape Thinking Traps

There are many ways that we limit our thinking. In an exercise called the "Thinking Trap," an escape route is found.

Individual Process (25 minutes): Draw a large square on a journal page. It will represent a Thinking Trap.

Start with the idea that your approach to teaching is confined and that you have accepted the confinement. Write brief responses to the following questions inside the trap.

What creative approaches to teaching have you:

■ Excluded from consideration because of your beliefs?

■ Banned because of unwritten rules or people's expectations?

■ Prohibited because of the story you tell about yourself as a person?

■ Omitted because they seem too risky?

■ Not allowed yourself to imagine?

Having discovered how your thinking is limited, escape the trap by creating at least two novel ideas for teaching. Feel the exhilaration of pursuing new approaches that have not occurred to you before. Expand your creative reach.

If you are working with a partner or group, share what you learned and created.

As teachers, we may be afraid that others will judge us harshly if we become too creative. This fearful thought will function like a training tether, holding us back from living more creative lives as teachers. When it occurs to us that we are holding ourselves back, we can cut the tether and free our minds. When we do, teaching becomes more fascinating.

Use Imagination

One of the most important "fun-da-mentals" of creativity is imagination. Why it is not used more widely in teaching is surprising, since it is a rich resource available to everyone. There are many ways to stimulate imagination, including exercises where students close their eyes to explore an issue from the perspective of another person, imagine the long-term consequences of a change, or create a new invention.

Creative Spirit:
*"Imagination is the ability to see what
has not yet become reality.
What can't be seen, can't be created."*

Individual Process (20 minutes): Think of a subject you will teach. Relying on the playful part of your mind, invent a learning exercise where you use the imagination of your students as a source of discovery. What will you have them imagine so they develop useful insights?

Cultivation: Take a moment to close your eyes and contemplate imagination. Reflect on its nature and how you will nourish it your students and in your teaching.

If you are working with a partner or group, share your ideas.

Imagine being able to think spontaneously about anything. What changes did you make within yourself to create that ability?

Imagine using that spontaneity to refresh your teaching and invent new ways of reaching and engaging your students in active learning.

Creative Spirit:
*"Imagine that you are the person
whose ideas you are teaching."*

Creative Side Trip

Let the creative spirit enter your teaching

When we establish creativity as the starting point in our teaching, we bring a new spirit of innovation into education. In what specific realms of teaching will you expand your creativity? What will you try?

Where I will expand my creativity in teaching:

What I will try:

Chapter 4

You Have Special Gifts

*A*s teachers, we are gifted in unique ways. Patience may be a gift or perhaps the capacity to listen carefully. Some of our gifts might be neglected. Others may have been put away, like children's toys that we think we have outgrown. Teachers, parents, and friends may have discouraged the use of our creative powers after childhood. In comparing our creative results to those of others, our own harsh judgments might have led us to hold back our creativity. For many of us, it is easier to acknowledge other people's special gifts than our own. By recognizing our gifts as teachers, we are more able to capitalize on them.

Creative Spirit:
"A carpenter doesn't arbitrarily select just any tool,
but chooses the one best suited for the purposes at hand.
Use your personal gifts in teaching
with that same clarity."

Gifts Are Tools

Personal gifts are tools for building a creative life as a teacher. What full range of gifts are available to you?

Individual Process (15 minutes): Divide a journal page in half.

In one part, record gifts you have for teaching. Perhaps you speak well or have the ability to develop rapport with your students. Circle your most important gifts. Put a star by those that consistently produce good results when you use them.

Take a leading gift and briefly describe how you will use it consciously to expand your creative reach as a teacher.

In the second part, note gifts you could develop for teaching if you spend time cultivating them. Circle those you would like to develop.

Examine the potential gifts you circled. Select one you would like to cultivate. Briefly describe steps you will take to develop it. Consider how you will use it to expand your creativity as a teacher.

New Possibilities: What new choices in teaching appear as you consider your personal gifts? Take a few minutes of silence to reflect on them.

If you are working with a partner or group, share what you discovered and what you will change.

Creative Spirit:
*"Teach as if you had the best qualities
of your favorite pet.
What would you do differently?"*

Retrieving Gifts From Childhood

One way to expand creativity in teaching is to reclaim what made us creative as young children. We can resurrect abilities from childhood that counteract our tendency to be too cautious and too serious as teachers today.

Individual Process (30 minutes): In your imagination, return to the time when you were about seven years old. If that was a difficult period in your life, go to a time when your creativity was more fully alive.

Being that age again, remember the things you liked to do. Notice how you were creative during play. Remember creative abilities you had that were lost or diminished in power through your years of education and self-assessment. Note those gifts on a journal page.

Remember your favorite toy or game as a child. Imagine yourself using that toy or playing that game. What creative abilities did the toy or game bring out in you? Imagination? The freedom to use your voice in many interesting ways?

Spontaneity? Add those abilities to your childhood gifts.

Using those gifts as creativity tools,

■ Identify one change you will make in your approach to teaching.

■ Note one thing you are now willing to try.

■ Record a new idea for an experiential exercise that will engage your students in active learning.

If you are working with a partner or group, share your childhood gifts and how you will use them in teaching now.

You are now more fully aware of your creative resources for teaching.

How will you use them to invent new ways of teaching, so you are more enthusiastic about education and students are more actively involved as learners?

How will you use them to realize your dreams as a teacher?

Creative Spirit:
*"Think of your mind as if it were
a painting by Joan Miro or Marc Chagall.
How would that mind view it?"*

Chapter 5

Engage Students In Active Learning

*E*xperiential teaching is based on the proverb: "Tell me and I'll forget. Show me and I'll learn. Involve me and I'll understand." When students experience ideas, not just hear or read about them, they become more active learners. Their understanding deepens as they discover for themselves the importance and complexity of a crucial issue. For example, instead of having students discuss the power of peer group pressure, create a learning exercise that will give them an experience of it. What interesting explorations and insights might emerge from their experience?

Creative Spirit:
"What new ideas for teaching would appear if you thought about your topic as a detective?
A hair stylist? A rock star? A saint?
An alien from another planet?"

Individual Process (40 minutes): "Roleing Around" is a creative technique that surprises the mind, so novel ideas emerge spontaneously. You examine a topic from unusual points of view to reveal unexpected insights.

How "Roleing Around" works. You begin by writing distinctively different social roles on six slips of paper. For example, "comedian" and "police officer" might come to mind. When the six roles are noted, turn the slips face down, so each role will be chosen randomly. Random selection surprises the mind so creative ideas come quickly.

After creating the roles, you identify a topic to teach by noting it on a large piece of paper. To begin, you randomly select a role. Putting yourself in the role, you draw on playful mind to generate new ideas or approaches to your topic, noting them as you go along. When you are ready for a shift of perspective, you choose a different role and repeat the process. Try a third or fourth role to discover what novel ideas they awaken in you. Using the ideas generated from "Roleing Around," you would develop an experiential exercise that actively engages your students in learning.

As an example, suppose your topic is "popularity." The role you choose is "architect." Engage playful mind by asking: "Taking the perspective of an architect, what ideas would I develop about popularity?" You might think about a "blueprint" for creating popularity, its vulnerability and breaking points, or what makes it more durable. Those ideas would be noted, along with others that come to mind as you think from the perspective of an architect. From those ideas, a learning exercise could be designed where small groups of students are assigned the task of creating a blueprint for how people could achieve and maintain popularity. What students create would lead to a deep exploration of the social construction of popularity.

Assuming the next role, you choose is "clown." What could

you learn about popularity by taking the role of a clown? Putting yourself in the clown's role, ideas emerge quickly. "Popularity is a dramatic performance, in the same way that my clown's costume, make-up, and funny antics convey the appearance of lighthearted play while covering up a more serious aspect of reality." From this idea alone, a learning process could be created where students design clothing, hair styles, make-up, and behaviors that would make someone more popular in the eyes of others. This exercise could lead to an exploration of popularity as a social drama of competing fashions within popular culture. How popularity is affected by presentation of self and what it forces people to hide about themselves would be key issues.

With these examples in mind, begin your own work. Tear a piece of paper into six parts. On each slip, note a social role, choosing roles that offer different perspectives. Turn the slips over and mix them.

On a large piece of paper, note a topic you will cover in your teaching.

Randomly select a social role. Imagining yourself in the role, let new ideas about your topic come to mind. Avoid judging the ideas. Instead, be open to unusual possibilities. Jot those down.

When the first role has exhausted its creative possibilities, select another and repeat the idea-generating process. Note those ideas. After a few minutes, select a third role to see what novel ideas it might inspire. Add them to your work.

When you have enough ideas, circle your leading prospects then design an experiential exercise that will actively involve your students in the issue.

When your creative work is finished, close your eyes. See

yourself employing the experiential process you created. Contemplate changes in classroom dynamics as you teach that way. How will using experiential exercises alter your students' motivation to participate and learn? How will it change your feelings about teaching?

If you are working with a partner or group, share your topics, ideas, and designs.

Creative Spirit:
"What could you learn from an automobile mechanic, an astronaut, or a bus driver about teaching?"

Alternative Process for Partners or a Group (40 minutes): Use "Roleing Around" with a partner or group of teachers. Agree on a topic to teach, a new project, a problem to solve, or a change of program to design. When the topic is established, record roles on separate slips of paper, turn them over, then randomly select one. Imagining yourselves in that role, co-create ideas together, recording your ideas as you go. When you need more inspiration, select another role and repeat the process. When you have enough ideas, circle your best prospects, then sketch out a design together.

How will you get your students directly involved in the topics you teach? What experiences will you create to draw them fully into participation so they become active learners?

Teaching experientially develops with practice. In time, creative ideas for exercises come quickly to mind.

How will you develop that ability?

What first steps will you take?

Creative Spirit:
"Pretend you're a gardener
of intellectually awakened minds.
What will you do to cultivate curiosity and excitement
in the minds of your students?"

Creative Side Trip

Make up quotes

Spontaneously making up your own quotes to write on the board is one way to bring the creative spirit to teaching. While employing learning processes in teaching, use the time students are working on their own to create a quote for the board that relates to that day's issues. Use the quote to stimulate students' thinking. Think of a topic that you will teach, then make up a quote which is:

Thought-provoking:

Humorous:

Surprising:

Imaginative:

Add quote making to your teaching. Notice how it makes teaching more interesting for you and your students.

Chapter 6

Be Willing To Take Risks

"*I*'m concerned about how others will respond to my creative efforts. Will I lose respect or have to pay a price?" This type of response appears quite often in my workshops when I ask teachers what stops them from being more creative. These concerns are examples of fear that make us cautious about becoming innovators. Other fears arise from questions about our abilities, our reluctance to risk failure, and the threat of looking bad or being punished.

Fearful thoughts have power over us because they tend to exaggerate the worst possible outcomes. They scare us because we think their exaggerated claims are true. By realizing that fearful thoughts are usually magnified, we learn to manage our fears so our creativity can develop more fully.

One semester, I observed a teacher who wanted to improve his effectiveness. He was a bright and engaging teacher who lectured from extensive notes, while offering occasional questions for discussion. While I listened to his lecture, I realized how much more compelling his ideas would be if he set up visual demonstrations to illustrate the physical principles he was teaching. Afterwards, I asked him if he ever used demonstrations. I assumed this was standard practice in his field, so I was surprised by his response. He said that he was reluctant to use them because he felt that he would be criticized by his colleagues for "catering to students." He wanted to avoid being seen as "another of those soft professors." For him, a narrow lecture and discussion format seemed the only legitimate way to teach. It also seemed the surest way to preserve his reputation.

I suggested that demonstrations would make his teaching more interesting and effective. It would add the necessary visual component to learning so students could quickly grasp the physical principles he was teaching. He welcomed my advice, saying "You mean, it's okay to do that kind of thing?" He was living in a fearful story about existing social norms and how his colleagues would judge him. The story was stopping him from doing the one thing in his classes that could dramatically increase his effectiveness. When we parted, he said he would start using demonstrations. My support for this innovation was all that he needed.

Creative Spirit:
"To put more adventure into your teaching,
try taking down your safety net."

Individual Process (25 minutes): On a journal page, record fears that inhibit your creativity as a teacher.

Circle your major fears.

What percentage of the time have your major fears come true? Note a percentage.

Most teachers learn from this exercise that their fears have been realized in a remarkably low percentage of the time, often 1% or less. Most of their fears have never come true. When fears are seen as exaggerations, choice and change emerge as possibilities. Apply the "1% rule" anytime a fear arises. Experience the fear, then realize that it is likely to materialize in 1% or less of the time. This shrinks the fear down to fit in the palm of your hand. Being so small, it is easier to use one of your personal resources, like courage or curiosity, to keep your creativity going.

Which of your many personal resources would allow you to stay in creative momentum when a fear is present? Note them. Circle two resources you will use in the face of fear.

Take one of your major fears. Apply the 1% rule so the fear fits in the palm of your hand, then, drawing on your personal resource, invent a creative idea for teaching. Using your playful mind, push through a boundary in your thinking in order to try something new. Have some fun!

Deeper Thinking: Take several minutes to reflect on the nature of your fears and how they limit what you are willing to try in teaching. Think more deeply about your capacity to control those fears so you can be more innovative.

If you are working with a partner or group, share your fears, discoveries, and what you are now willing to create as a teacher.

Creative Spirit:
*"Instead of fearing that things will go wrong,
teach today as if everything will go right."*

Alternative Process for a Group (30 minutes): Meet in a room with a large chalk board. Ask the participants to note fears that inhibit their creativity as teachers on a piece of paper. When they have completed that task, ask for volunteers to write one of their major fears on the left side of the board. When the board is full of fears, ask members of the group: "How do these fears stop us from being more creative teachers?" After hearing their responses, ask: "What is the realistic probability those fears will come true?" Focusing on a few fears, have people suggest percentages. Note them next to each fear. Introduce the 1% rule and how to use it.

On the right side of the board, invite volunteers to record personal resources they could use to maintain their creativity when fear tries to stop them.

Ask everyone to select a fear and a resource from the board. Invite them to apply the 1% rule to the fear, then use the resource they chose from the board to push through the fear and develop a creative idea for teaching.

Have volunteers record their new teaching ideas in the middle of the board. Ask them to share how they managed their fears so they could create new ideas.

End with a general discussion of fear and how to stay in creative momentum as teachers.

Managing Fears

By realizing that fearful thoughts are usually exaggerations, we develop the ability to control our fears rather than being automatically under their influence. When a fearful thought emerges, the 1% rule and our own resources can keep us in creative momentum. If that fails to work, we can use one of the "Three Rs," which are decisions for managing any negative thought.

We can:

■ Reject the negative thought. For example, "I can't do it" is discarded.
■ Reverse it, so it becomes positive. "I can do it."
■ Replace it with any positive thought of your choice. "With patience and practice, I know I can learn how to do this."

When fearful and other negative thoughts are brought under control, we expand our capacity to explore new ground as teachers.

Creative Spirit:
"Try putting your fears on the run instead of being run by them."

Individual Process (10 minutes): Select three fears. State each fear out loud, then apply one of the "Three R" decisions to put a stop to it. Reject it, reverse it, or replace it. Experience your ability to manage your fearful thoughts, so your creativity flourishes.

Alternative Process for Partners or a Group (15 minutes): After selecting three fears, sit with a partner. Taking turns, share a fear, then, speaking aloud, use each of the Three R decisions to manage them. Discuss what you learned.

Creative Spirit:
"Think of your fears as bad dreams
that never come true.
What will you be willing to try in teaching now?"

As teachers, more possibilities for creativity are available than our fears would lead us to believe. To discover the full range of those possibilities, push through the boundaries of convention and watch for results and responses. If you carry teaching innovations out in a reasonable way, you will discover that your fears of being criticized and punished were exaggerated. It is more likely that your teaching will become more effective as you expand your creativity. It is difficult for others to argue against success.

As you cultivate a more creative way to think and be, it will affect your teaching and how you live. At that point, playfulness will enter your life to add flexibility, originality, and fun to whatever you do. "What is the creative thing to think and do?" will become your first and guiding question. From that simple question, imagine the discoveries you will make and the new teaching methods you will try. Instead of a proving ground, imagine that your life is a playground.

Creative Spirit:
"Instead of thinking 'play it safe',
think 'play is safe'."

Chapter 7

Manage The Size Of Your Ego

$\mathcal{M}$onica was busy pulling her materials together after class when one of her students came to her and said with enthusiasm, "I want you to know what a tremendous impact your teaching is having on me. It's shifting the way I think about myself." The session had gone well and her student's comment elevated Monica's mood. She left the classroom feeling happy and fulfilled.

Meredith was filling in for another teacher who had to be out of town. It was a subject she was teaching, so she knew the material well. She thought it would be fun. As she was teaching, a small group of young men kept whispering to each other and laughing quietly in the back row. Feeling the rejection, she quickly became very upset, but she was unsure about how to respond to them. Their rudeness caught her completely off guard. With her confidence undermined, she began speaking rapidly and forcefully, pushing her points across likes bullets. At the end she was drained, upset, and hurt. She left the classroom feeling that the session had been a "complete disaster."

These experiences reveal how teaching can alter the size of our egos. A compliment can quickly enlarge our egos and make us feel wonderful; disrespect or criticism can quickly deflate them and ruin our day. Every teacher has stories to tell about these good and bad feeling times. It does not take much effort to remember a session that went well beyond measure or one that was a disaster. Remember the compliment from a student that created good feelings or a criticism that cut to the core? Being human, most teachers have egos that are inherently vulnerable to deflation or collapse.

Creative Spirit:
"A deflated ego will undermine teaching as fast as a five dollar bill disappears from a sidewalk."

Imagine that the human ego is a balloon which constantly expands and contracts as it responds to compliments and criticisms, successes and failures. For teachers, its size is apt to decrease when we have

> looked foolish,
> lost control,
> lost respect,
> were ineffective,
> or made a mistake.

Any one of these experiences, if severe enough, can make a good teacher feel small, disappointed, and depressed. When the ego deflates while teaching, confidence may decline so rapidly that it feels like emotional drowning. Feeling suddenly weak and inadequate, the volume and speed of our delivery may automatically increase to cover up our helpless feelings. As we teach, there is a part of us that hopes students will not notice the cover up. On the contrary, when we are able to maintain control, gain respect, and achieve satisfaction, our ego expands, so we automatically feel big and good. In that elevated ego state, we teach with confidence, even bravado. Those are the good teaching days.

Teachers Have Vulnerable Egos Too

Largely unaware of it, teachers are constantly managing the size of their egos. They try to be big enough to feel good about themselves and the day. They avoid situations that might cause their egos to deflate or collapse. The negative impact of these human tendencies on education and classroom dynamics is obvious. Ego fears can lead teachers to avoid taking creative risks and students to be reluctant participants rather than fully engaged learners. Afraid of failure and ridicule, students manage their ego size by holding back or expressing ideas they think will be acceptable to the teacher and their peers.

When teachers and students take the safe route, education becomes careful and confined. Freedom of expression may become a dream no one wants to realize because it is too risky. When people are afraid, creativity is curtailed.

Individual Process (20 minutes): Anything that has the potential to deflate your ego, you will fear and therefore avoid.

Which of the following ego concerns do you fear most as a teacher? Check them.

☐ Looking foolish.
☐ Losing control.
☐ Losing respect.
☐ Being ineffective.
☐ Making a mistake.

Taking each of the ego fears you checked, describe what

you do to avoid it so you can maintain a comfortable ego size.

Note how those strategies hold you back from becoming a more creative teacher. What do you avoid trying because it seems too threatening to your ego?

With that awareness, what new choices are possible?

What are you willing to try now?

If you are working with a partner or group, share your discoveries.

Why is it that in the midst of positive feedback from students, one negative comment about our teaching can ruin a day? The comment may become an obsessive preoccupation late into the night. When the disappointment is acute, depression may overwhelm us to a point where giving up teaching may seem like a good idea. Those are the times when our fragile egos have temporarily deflated, so negative thinking automatically emerges to torment us. We eventually recover from those troubling moods when a compliment or a good day of teaching help us out of our ego ruts.

Creative Spirit:
"When your ego feels little,
your mind will be more reluctant to play."

A "Recovery Claim" Is An Ego Saver

Using a "Recovery Claim" can help to restore the size of our egos during or following a disappointing class or after receiving a criticism. A claim is a positive belief we hold about ourselves that we know is true. "I'm a good person" or "I'm good enough" are examples. While having a disappointing experience while teaching, "I'm good enough" is the statement I make to myself in order to restore my ego's size. The claim keeps me in balance, so I can maintain my confidence and effectiveness.

Individual Process (15 minutes): On a journal page, write Recovery Claims you could use when circumstances cause your ego to deflate. Include "I'm good enough" or "I'm a good person," if those claims are true for you.

Review the ego fears that you checked in the last process. Taking each fear, briefly describe the circumstances which would lead your ego to deflate. Would it be something you said or did? Something students said or did? Be specific.

Close your eyes and recall one of those ego-deflating situations. As you imagine it, use a Recovery Claim to stop your ego from shrinking. How does stating the claim help you to restore your balance and effectiveness?

Imagine yourself in another situation that would cause ego deflation. Use a different Recovery Claim to restore your ego's size. Notice how it helps you to recover your balance and effectiveness.

Try a third claim in another situation. Notice what happens.

Which claim works best for you?

How and when will you use it as a practice?

If you are working with a partner or group, discuss the Recovery Claim you found most useful. Describe how and when you will use it.

Notice how your circumstances and the statements of others affect the size of your ego. It probably enlarges when you are effective or receive a compliment and deflates when your teaching falters or you receive a criticism. In any given day, the size of your ego may change several times, often in very subtle ways, but also dramatically when your results are extremely positive or negative. This is why you may experience teaching as a roller coaster ride. The dramatic swings from high to low are your ego expanding and contracting. By using a Recovery Claim, you will achieve a higher degree of internal control and stability, so you can avoid falling helplessly into depressing moods that undermine your motivation and effectiveness.

Creative Spirit:
"When you feel your confidence declining,
use a Recovery Claim to blow air into
your shrinking ego."

Self-Criticism

Other peoples' criticisms can deflate us, but so can our own negative judgments. Our inner judge may launch such harsh criticisms of our teaching that we make ourselves miserable. Getting to know our condemning judge is important for responding to its many complaints rather than being at its mercy. There is a difference between employing internal criticism as feedback to change what we are doing and using it to torture ourselves.

Individual Process (15 minutes): At the top of a journal page, put "Condemnations of my inner judge." Note comments your judge has made about you and your teaching which have diminished your confidence and undermined your effectiveness.

Circle the self-criticisms that have the biggest impact on your ego.

With your eyes closed, visit a leading criticism. As you imagine how your ego might deflate under the weight of that judgment, establish a Recovery Claim to stop its collapse. Feel yourself managing the size of your ego.

Take another criticism. Realize it is just a thought. With your eyes closed, imagine your ego deflating, then use one of the Three Rs:

Reject the thought.
Reverse the thought to make it positive.
Replace it will any positive thought you choose.

If you are working with a partner or group, share what you discovered.

Teachers are always on the line. We are open to compliments and criticisms from others and our inner judges. We have good and bad teaching days. Most of us are unaware of how automatically we react to these messages and circumstances, sometimes feeling inflated and good, while, at other times, we are overcome by deflation and defeat.

Now that you are aware of how these ego dynamics work, you can consciously intervene with a Recovery Claim or the Three Rs to change your thinking. This will give you more internal control over the circumstances that would normally lower your self-confidence and effectiveness as a teacher.

Creative Side Trip

Make your teaching
more of an adventure

Most people think of risk as dangerous, rather than as an opportunity to discover what is possible. Risk is an indispensable part of any adventure, including teaching. With your new capacity to maintain a comfortable ego size, note new risks you are willing to take now.

Risk:

Risk:

Risk:

Instead of thinking that risks are dangerous, view them as essential for adding vitality to your teaching. Risk is where the adventure in teaching begins.

Chapter 8

Create Motivation
And Participation

*W*hen students show little motivation to learn, education loses its spirit, so teaching is a struggle rather than a pleasure. In the face of student indifference, it is easy to become resigned to the situation, putting in our time but withholding our hearts. The alternative approach is to treat motivation as something we have the power to create as teachers. When our commitment to motivate students is strong, our chances of success dramatically improve.

Creative Spirit:
"Motivate yourself.
On your way to class, declare the possibility that
you will create the most powerful learning experience
you have ever created as a teacher."

Individual Process (40 minutes): Recall a time when you felt highly motivated to learn. Focus your attention on the factors that motivated you. For example, curiosity might have been a factor or maybe you were excited by a challenge. On a journal page, note in a word or two the factors that increased your motivation.

Thinking more broadly, add other factors that motivate people to learn.

Examining your work, circle four of the most potent motivators.

Divide a page into quarters. Write one of the four motivators in each part. These will be your motivational cornerstones for teaching. Consider their importance in shaping what you do as a teacher.

Identify a topic you will teach. Moving from cornerstone to cornerstone, develop innovative ideas for an experiential learning exercise. Among the ideas in each part, add at least one that surprises you. Notice how each cornerstone stimulates unique ideas. For example, suppose one of your cornerstones is "significance." What new ideas for teaching your topic would appear if you started with the question "What are novel ways of giving students an experience of this topic's significance?"

When you have completed recording your ideas, circle the most promising ones.

Using those ideas, sketch out an experiential exercise for teaching your topic which builds on one or more of your motivational cornerstones. For example, if "curiosity" is one of your cornerstones, you would design the exercise with the intention of igniting your students' curiosity. If "challenge" is a cornerstone, you would create an experience that would challenge them to think in new ways about the topic. To build on both cornerstones, start by asking: "How can I design a process that will make students curious while also challenging them to think up new ideas?"

New Possibilities: How will knowledge of the cornerstones of motivation affect your teaching? Close your eyes and explore the possibilities.

If you are working with a partner or group, share your motivational cornerstones and teaching exercises.

When you focus on key motivational cornerstones before designing a learning process, you increase your chances of creating an exercise that will lead your students to participate. For example, if you know that a sense of "mystery" motivates people to learn, you can design an exercise using "mystery" as a motivational anchor. "How will I engage the minds of my students in the mysteries of this topic?" As soon as you raise the question, notice how your mind begins seeking novel answers.

Creative Spirit:
"What you don't go after, you won't get.
"You can create full participation in five minutes
if you have a clear intention to create it."

Motivation Does Not
Guarantee Participation

How many times have you encouraged students to participate with only marginal success? Even when students are motivated, they may not want to participate. Why do they hold back? Their participation is withheld because of an automatic chain reaction between their thinking, feelings, and behavior. It has three elements: Fear – insecurity – employment of a strategy to avoid ego deflation.

Group Process (30 minutes): To create greater awareness of why students are reluctant to participate, consider doing the following exercise with them. It might be used toward the beginning of a semester or when participation has fallen to such a low point that there is not enough vitality among them to nourish learning.

Start by saying: "In a moment, I'm going to invite one of you to the front of the room to share something meaningful about what you have learned in this class." If an eager hand goes up, avoid calling on that person by saying "I'll choose who will share in a moment." Maintain silence and observe how students avoid being chosen. Some will look away. Others might make direct eye contact with you in the hope that you will avoid calling on them because they look so eager.

Fear: Let a minute pass in silence as you look around the room. When the tension has become acute, ask: "What fears do you experience when I ask you to share?" Students may say "I'm afraid of looking foolish" or "I'm afraid I might say something I'll regret later." As an alternative, ask students to write their fears on the board. This is less threatening than speaking and it has the added value of being visible to all.

Insecurity: When the fears are known, ask: "What insecurities does participation create in you?" You may hear "I feel vulnerable because I'm afraid of rejection." As students describe their insecurities, listen for concerns about ego deflation and their automatic avoidance of feeling little and bad.

Strategy for avoiding ego deflation: "When you're feeling insecure, what strategy do you use to avoid having to participate?" This follow-up question will produce some interesting responses. "I sit in the back of the room, hoping you won't notice me." "I avoid eye contact with you." "I stare you down, praying you will call on someone who seems to be avoiding the challenge." Like us, students will automatically avoid circumstances that threaten to make them feel little and bad. Since participation presents that threat to so many of them, especially the introverted students, they will resist our efforts to encourage their participation, even when they feel motivated to learn. Afraid of making mistakes, looking foolish, or being criticized, they will automatically hold back to protect themselves from the negative feelings of ego deflation.

Conclude this exercise by asking: "What personal resources do you have that would allow you to participate in the face of fear?" Have your students share a resource they could employ. Consider asking them to write their key resources on the board so they can see the broad range of resources available to everyone. Ask for volunteers to share the resource they could use to act in the face of fear. If the class is small enough, consider having each student share a resource.

There is an important implication of this work for understanding the ways people participate in life. This can be pointed out, so students understand that the classroom can be a laboratory for changing how they live. Many of us fail to fully participate in life because of the chain reaction of fear–insecurity–employment of a strategy to avoid ego deflation. In the face of a threat, our strategy might be to become observers rather than active participants. What would our tombstones say? "Lived safely in the stands" or "Played boldly on the court?"

Which of these inscriptions describes you?

Which would describe your students? Ask them.

Individual Process (20 minutes): By understanding what makes students reticent to participate, you can create ways to invite them into a dialogue with you and each other.

On a journal page, note two changes that you will make in the way you communicate and behave as a teacher, with the following goals in mind:

■ The first change will reduce students' fear of participating.

■ The second will increase their security so they are freer to express their ideas honestly.

If you are working with a partner or group, share what you created.

My office was once connected to a classroom by a common wall. On the opening day of class one semester, I heard a teacher say, "I want you to know that I will welcome your ideas and participation as we confront the issues of this course together." This comment was made in a friendly, open way, so I thought to myself, "This is a teacher who knows how to invite students to participate." Then, suddenly, the teacher's tone became hard and controlling. "Yes, I want you to participate, but before you do, you must go to the library and prepare yourself to ask your question or make your statement. I won't tolerate unprepared thinking." A tense silence fell over the room, and it largely remained that way throughout the semester. His threat increased fear and insecurity, so only the bravest of students dared to share their views. "Afraid to speak up, so life couldn't appear there" would describe that teacher's course.

In sharp contrast, imagine people saying about your classes, "Everyone spoke freely. Life occurred there in abundance."

What did you do to create that atmosphere?

What will you do now?

Creative Spirit:
"How will you teach so you become
a good memory for your students?"

Chapter 9

Community Service
Stimulates Learning

Service learning integrates intellectual work in the classroom and service in the community. It is becoming an important part of education at all levels. By extending education into the community, students learn by becoming immersed in community issues and problem-solving. This immersion experience elevates their interest and motivation to learn.

Service-learning courses work well in a variety of fields. There is a service-learning course in Engineering at my university where students learn engineering skills while serving senior citizens by designing inventions to help with their mobility problems. Students from the sciences can serve in community organizations that deal with health or environmental issues. In the social sciences, they can volunteer to work in community agencies that serve people whose lives are adversely affected by social problems. In the languages, service-learning opportunities exist to tutor people who are learning a second language.

To enrich the education of your students and enliven your teaching, design a new service-learning course or add a community service component to an existing course to give it a service-learning emphasis.

Creative Spirit:
*"Expand the size of your classroom
to include your local community,
then expand it to include the world."*

Visiting the Dream, Planning,
And Critic's Rooms

To design or modify any course, visit the three rooms of
Walt Disney Studios to improve your chances of success:
The Dream Room, the Planning Room, and the Critic's
Room. These are separate and distinctive rooms. In the
dream room, imagination is honored. After a dream is identified, it is imagined in detail. Then, it is taken into the planning room, where a strategy is designed to implement it.
Afterwards, the critic's room is visited. The role of criticism is to refine the plan to increase its chances of success.
Based on the nature of the criticism, the planning or dream
room may be revisited for further work.

Individual Process (60 minutes): Have a large piece of
paper on hand. Prepare to dream, plan, and criticize.

The Dream Room. Imagine a service-learning course that
you would enjoy teaching, either a new course you create or
an existing one modified to include community service.
With your eyes closed, imagine how the service and learning components would work together to create a powerful
educational experience for your students. Then imagine the

impact service learning would have on the interest level of students, their involvement in the intellectual content of the course, and their willingness to participate in classroom discussions. Dream up the course in as much detail as possible, then go to the next room.

The Planning Room. Imagine that you are in a room where your instincts for planning are fully alive. Based on what you imagined in the dream room, you will design your service learning course in detail. As you create the course, consider the following questions:

■ What are your teaching objectives? What do you want students to learn from a service-learning course?

■ What innovations in learning are possible when community service is an integral part of your course? How will you include them in your plan?

■ How will you balance your students' community service with their classroom work? How much service will you expect? Where will the service occur?

■ How will you integrate what students learn from their community service into the academic content of the course?

■ How will you use the academic content to help illuminate for students what they are learning about community issues?

■ What will you evaluate in the course? What weight will you assign to required activities?

Design your course with these and other questions in mind. Develop a detailed plan, then move into the next room.

The Critic's Room. Imagine an inner critic who is capable of refining your plan to make it more effective. Invite that critic to evaluate your plan and offer recommendations for change. Modify your plan accordingly.

When your plan is revised, note the semester when you will first teach the course. Then, identify steps you will take today or tomorrow to begin working toward that goal.

If you are working with a partner or group, share your plans and discuss your ideas.

Creative Spirit:
"Feel like a servant when you teach.
Whom are you serving? What are you serving?"

When a course includes community service, the interest and involvement of your students will expand beyond the classroom. As they gain direct experience of an issue in the community, you will see a dramatic rise in their motivation and receptivity to learn, accompanied by a greater willingness to make a contribution to community change and classroom discussions. By combining learning and service in your teaching, theory and practice come together around tangible concerns students care about, so their educational experience becomes richer for them. Learning about their community and its problems also teaches them the value of civic responsibility, which is a benefit in its own right.

Chapter 10

Cultivate Inspiration

*M*oments of inspiration awaken the mind to new possibilities. There is no need to wait for those flashes of insight, because they can be created by using "inspiration points" to surprise your mind. Anything can be an inspiration point: Courage, joy, awe, a flower, a bird, a song, or love. The activity of the mind will be shaped by the inspiration point we choose. Imagine preparing a learning process about the women's suffrage movement using the inspiration point "eye."

What thoughts would arise by letting our minds play with that simple image? How did the suffrage movement open women's eyes to injustice? What was seen that had not been fully recognized before? Some people believe the eye is an opening to the soul. What was the soul of the suffrage movement? How was it nourished? What part did it play in generating and perpetuating women's involvement even in the face of risks to themselves and their families? What ideas would emerge by focusing on the mobility of the eyes? How did the increasing mobility of women affect the growth and vitality of the movement? With "eye" as a source of inspiration, three angles on the movement quickly appear that could be the basis for an experiential exercise. Working from inspiration points, let your mind play with the images to spark new ideas. What you create may surprise you.

Creative Spirit:
"Cultivate inspiration and watch
the creativity garden grow."

Individual Process (30 minutes): At the top of a journal page, note a topic you will teach.

Divide the page into four parts. In each part, write an inspiration point. The first four things that come to mind will do. They can be attributes such as courage, feelings like love, objects like the sun, or experiences like a great vacation.

Start with one of your inspiration points. Let the playful part of your mind generate ideas about your topic and how it might be taught in a creative way. Note those ideas.

Go to your next inspiration point. Generate and record new ideas.

Move to the remaining two inspiration points and repeat the idea-generating process. Stretch beyond the limits of conventional thinking.

Circle your most promising ideas in each section.

From those ideas, sketch out an experiential exercise for

teaching your topic.

Cultivation: Where will you cultivate the use of inspiration points in your teaching? With eyes closed, contemplate the opportunities.

If you are working with a partner or group, share what you learned and created.

Inspiration points are like splashing cold water on the mind. They awaken its spirit and encourage creative thinking. This adds adventure to any assignment. Where you feel stale or stuck, inspiration points will automatically startle your mind, so new ideas will emerge with little effort. Water is added to dry land, so things begin to grow again.

Creative Spirit:
"Be inspired by your students today."

We Live In Pictures

As teachers, most of us are unaware that we live within metaphors, or mental pictures. "Proving ground" may be our guiding metaphor. Without knowing it, these pictures affect our teaching and how we feel about it. Depending on their content, the images can inspire or depress us.

One semester, I worked with a teacher who was looking for a change. At our first meeting, he described how miserable teaching made him feel. I asked him what picture he was living within when he taught. Caught by surprise, he had to think about it for a moment, then said, as if a light were going on in his mind, "A prisoner of war camp." Seeing this picture helped him discover what was making him feel trapped, undernourished, hopeless, and drained of spirit.

When the problem had been deeply explored, I asked:

"What's the picture you'd like to live in as a teacher?"

"A surfboard" was his immediate response.

"How would that picture transform your teaching?" I asked.

"To ride on a surfboard you need balance and, once you achieve that, you can have some fun."

He talked about how he could achieve more balance in his teaching and what it would be like to have fun teaching while pursuing issues that meant a lot to him.

Over the semester, he used the image of a "surfboard" to change what he was doing in the classroom. By the end of the term, he had created a more balanced approach and was having more fun. Two years later when we spoke, he was still enjoying teaching. By simply changing his picture, he altered his life as a teacher.

Individual Process (20 minutes): What is the dominant picture you live within as a teacher?

Jot down ideas, and put a circle around your most dominant image. Describe how it affects what you do as a teacher and how you feel about teaching.

If your picture is nourishing, describe how you might use it more consciously as a stimulus for innovation.

If your picture fails to nurture you, identify other pictures you might try. Select one that you think could make a positive difference. Describe how it would change your attitude, your approach to teaching, and what you would try.

If you are working with a partner or group, share your discoveries.

"'Computer' is the picture I teach within." This was the discovery of a young woman in one of my teaching workshops. The computer image helped her see a problem in her teaching: "I tend to teach in a cold and calculated way, like a computer. I have to have everything under my control."

"What is the picture you'd like to teach within?" I asked.

"What about a computer with a blanket over it?" she said, and everyone laughed.

"What would that do for you?" another teacher asked.

"The blanket would add some warmth to the cold, careful side of me. I probably can't help being organized, but I'm missing the possibility of warmer relationships with my students. A computer with a blanket over it opens up an opportunity to make that change."

Creative Spirit:
"For one day, teach within the
picture of a sunny, springtime day
when the blossoms are at the peak of their beauty.
On another, teach as a bolt of lightening."

Chapter 11

Develop Novel Ideas For Teaching

When determined to explore, we discover fresh ideas most quickly by taking unusual routes. Pick up an aluminum can and let it be the source of inspiration about any topic. To quickly shift perspectives, visit someone else's mind. Caught by surprise, the mind is encouraged to look for new ideas. "Object Play" and "Mind Switching" stimulate its search.

Creative Spirit:
"To awaken new ideas,
surprise the mind."

Objects Are Thinking Toys

Object Play stimulates new ideas that lead to unique learning exercises. Imagine your topic is social conflict and you have picked up a set of keys. Inviting your mind to play with the keys like a toy, a series of questions come quickly to mind. "What are the key ideas for unraveling the mystery of social conflict? What is the nature of the mystery? What crimes are involved? Who are the suspects? What is the evidence?" Using these questions, you would design an experiential exercise that would ask students to investigate social conflict as a mystery to unlock.

Object play is also useful for stimulating the creativity of students. Have your students use objects to generate their own ideas about social conflict. Teach from their discoveries. By adding a greater variety of creative approaches to your teaching, you keep everyone's mind in a surprised and stimulated state. This keeps the minds of the students in the room, as opposed to excursions outside when, having lost interest, they fall into day dreaming.

Creative Spirit:
"Create variety in your teaching today.
Notice how much you enjoy it."

Individual Process (30 minutes): Note a classroom topic in the middle of a journal page. Collect four objects within easy reach. Make them small enough so you can hold them in your hands. Pockets and purses are often fertile hunting grounds. Place the objects in front of you.

Pick up an object. Exploring its many facets, let your mind play off what you see and feel to generate novel ideas for teaching your topic. Write those ideas down. Select another object and repeat the process. Try a third to discover its creative potential.

When you have a reasonable number of interesting ideas, circle your best prospects. With your topic in mind, use your ideas to design an experiential exercise that will engage the minds of your students.

If you are working with a partner or group, share your ideas and designs.

Creative Spirit:
"For one day, be the 1/4 inch of whipped cream that makes the hot chocolate taste so good. How will you teach in a special way?"

Visit Someone Else's Mind

It is easy to fall into familiar patterns of thinking out of habit or as a way of avoiding the anxiety of taking risks. To develop new ideas, we leave the comfort of what is known and accepted to enter uncharted territory in our minds. Object play encourages this more risky venture by shifting our perspective. Another way to expand our thinking is to visit another person's mind. Called "Mind Switching," the trip requires a leap of imagination.

Individual Process (30 minutes): At the top of a journal page, record a topic you will teach. Next, note the names of people whose minds you could visit to expand your thinking about the issue.

If your problem is peaceful coexistence, consider visiting

Mahatma Gandhi's mind to discover what he would add to your thinking. If you are looking for a novel way to teach students about a key scientific principle, visiting Einstein's mind might help you create a fresh approach. You could visit the mind of a friend whose perspective would challenge you to think in new ways. You could visit the mind of a clown or comedian to explore the lighter side of the issue. Consider mind visits that will help broaden your perspective and provide new ideas for teaching your topic.

From among your names, select a mind to visit.

With your eyes closed, switch into that person's mind in order to think about your topic in new ways. Imagine the questions that person might raise about the issue. What new avenues of thinking will be revealed? When your visit is over, note the ideas you received.

Using those ideas, design an engaging exercise for teaching your topic.

If you are working with a partner or group, share your experiences and designs.

Creative Spirit:
"For new ideas,
visit someone else's mind.
It's another kind of library."

Paul eventually undermine our enthusiasm for teaching

When we become too comfortable with our thinking patterns, teaching styles, or subject matter, repetition and boredom may drain the life from our teaching. Emphasizing creativity nurtures a spark of vitality so we can avoid or escape those teaching ruts. The principle "always searching, creating, and changing" keeps the creative spirit alive in teaching.

Contemplate a rut you are in as a teacher.

What escape routes do you see?

How could you use a can opener as a source of inspiration to find a way out?

Would a visit to the mind of a higher intelligence in another galaxy be helpful?

Creative Spirit:
"What can you add to teaching
so it bubbles up rather than dries up?"

Creative Side Trip

Challenges inspire students

Students enjoy and respond to challenges. I discovered this while teaching a very large introductory course over several years. At take-home exam time, I would ask students to raise their hands if they were willing to take on the challenge of writing the best essay that they had ever written. Typically, about 20 per cent of the students raised their hands. I then spoke to those students directly, encouraging their effort and inspiring them to do their best work. I asked them to tell me what difference they noticed in their commitment and the quality of their work. Later, many were eager to tell me how it inspired them and how proud they were of the quality of the work they had done. Challenges can make a difference when they are made to a whole class or to individual students. Under the following, write a challenge that will inspire:

Excellence:

Creativity:

Full self-expression:

Change:

Chapter 12

Nurture Positive Relationships

*M*aking up stories about students is inevitable. What we say about them arises from our day-to-day experience as teachers. Some of us tell generally positive stories; others repeat more negative ones. Those stories shape our interpretations of students' motives and behavior. They affect what we look for and see. The quality of our relationships with students, how we teach, and how we feel about teaching are influenced by the nature of our stories.

Creative Spirit:
"Stories imprison the mind.
When you question your stories, you break free,
then new ideas and choices appear as if by magic."

Individual Process (10 minutes): On a journal page, put "Students are. . . ." Around the page, complete the sentence by recording the first words that come to mind. Identify positive and negative judgments that capture the fullness and complexity of your story.

Examine the words you wrote as beliefs you hold about students. Underline the important beliefs, both positive and negative. Using those beliefs as plot material, sketch out the story you tell yourself or others about your students. Afterwards, give it a title that captures its essence.

In what specific ways does your story affect the quality of your relationships with students and how you teach? How does it influence your level of trust in them? Your willingness to respect and show concern for them? Note insights.

Now that you are more aware of the effects of your story, note any changes you would like to make in it. What beliefs will you exclude, add, or modify?

With those changes in mind, edit your story and give it a new title.

Contemplate the new possibilities for teaching that emerge from your revisions.

If you are working with a partner or group, share your discoveries.

Over many years of teaching, I have heard a significant number of teachers convey negative stories about their students. "They're lazy." "All they care about are grades." "They aren't very bright." "All they want to do is party." At times, I wondered why the negative story tellers continued to teach, for complaints had replaced their initial excitement for teaching. Had they been willing to question their stories, they might have renewed their enthusiasm for teaching. In contrast, teachers who create positive stories about students are apt to have students with positive stories about them because they will teach with more warmth, enthusiasm, and commitment.

When I was a new teacher, I worried about students deceiving me. I lived in a story that they would lie and cheat if I failed to keep my eye on them. This story made me suspicious. Over time, I discovered that my story was simply not true for the vast majority of my students, who had personal integrity and could be trusted.

I eventually realized that my negative story was diminishing my enjoyment of teaching because, expecting deceit, I had to live in a gloomy picture. Imagine taking a vacation where you think someone will grab your purse or pick your pocket at any moment. It would not be much of a vacation, because the constant suspicion would take much of the pleasure out of it. That was precisely what my negative story about students was doing to my enjoyment of teaching.

I acknowledged that I did have a few students who either took advantage of me or tried to deceive me when it was in their interest. But, it was such a small percentage, I wondered why I should mistrust the vast majority of students who were honest. So, I made a decision. Instead of thinking that lying and cheating were the rule, I would treat them as minor exceptions. I decided I would trust all my students and deal with any student who lied or cheated on an individual basis. This decision meant that I had to accept being duped by a few students in order to fully trust all the rest. If the dishonest students got away with something, I knew it would work against them in the long run and they would pay a price.

Making that decision was one of the best things I did for myself as a teacher. It gave me a positive story to live in that increased my enjoyment of teaching. Now students know that I trust them and expect trust to be a principle that exists between us. This shift toward trust has produced many positive and productive relationships with my students over the years.

Creative Spirit:
"Trust will never grow from suspicion.
Only trust can create trust."

Developing Rapport

During one of my teaching workshops, a young teacher confessed that, while she had a natural sense of humor, she withheld it for fear that it would undermine her authority. I asked her what she was sacrificing to gain that authority. "I'm not having much fun" was her quick reply. This realization forced her to consider what she would gain by bringing her natural playfulness out into the open while teaching. She wondered whether she could earn the respect of her students while also having more fun. She saw the possibility of balance. Before leaving the workshop, she had made a decision to lighten up by letting some of her humor out.

When teachers adhere rigidly to an image of authority, they may become so serious that they lose the possibility of fun which is inherent in teaching. They are also likely to establish greater social distance between themselves and their students, which reduces the possibility that good relation-ships will develop. When teachers share their doubts, sense of humor, mistakes, gaps in knowledge, and lives with students, a human connection is developed. From that connection, a learning community begins and grows.

Sharing ourselves honestly while teaching is an issue of balance. If we withhold too much of ourselves, students may feel that we are "distant and cold." When we reveal everything, they may lose respect for us. Create balance as part of the middle way.

Creative Spirit:
"Instead of trying to prove yourself,
share yourself."

Individual Process (15 minutes): What do you withhold about yourself while teaching? On a journal page, jot down the personal qualities and information that you hold back because you think they are at odds with your image, role, or authority. Maybe you cover up your mistakes or hold back your sense of humor. Do you love poetry, but keep it separate from your teaching? Is music a passion you keep hidden?

Examine what you have written. Circle any quality or fact that could be brought into your teaching, keeping the idea of balance in mind (not too much; not too little). Given what you identified, how could you change your image or change how you interpret your role and authority so you can share more of yourself with your students? Briefly note the changes.

If you are working with a partner or group, discuss what you discovered and what you will do to bring more of yourself into teaching.

Creative Spirit:
"Today, teach like a work of art
with many interesting dimensions."

Developing Four Ethical Principles

One way to improve relationships with students is to change the beliefs we hold about them and to change their beliefs about us by sharing more of ourselves. Another is to create ethical principles that determine how we treat them and how we want them to treat us and each other.

Individual Process (20 minutes): Divide a journal page into quarters. In each part, record an ethical principle that would shape:

> How you treat your students,
> how they treat you, and
> how they treat each other.

Revise your principles until they become a firm foundation

for developing positive relationships with and between students.

Visualize: With your eyes closed, see yourself teaching in harmony with your four principles. What effects do you notice?

If you are working with a partner or group, share your four principles and their possible impact.

Our students know when we trust them and genuinely care about their development. When they know, they will be more open to our teaching and advice. They also become more active participants in learning. When they believe we do not trust or care for them, they reciprocate by not trusting or caring for us, so the teacher-student relationship dissolves into one of control. In a relationship governed by domination and submission, power through giving grades is attained at the expense of the student's development and our own enjoyment of teaching.

Creative Spirit:
"Teach in a way that makes your students feel
like the fourth leg of a chair—necessary and important."

Chapter 13

Create Balance

$\mathcal{I}$n striving to become more creative, teachers may reject what they are doing and pursue the other extreme. This is chronicled in Jane Thompson's fascinating book, *A Life in School*. After years of teaching students in a conventional lecture and discussion format, she decided to step away from the lectern and let learning emerge through honest and deep communication. She set her concern with authority aside and abandoned a clear organizational structure in favor of community, spontaneity, and fuller self-expression. By going from one extreme to another, she felt guilty, fearful, and more sensitive to the opinions of others. Her book is excellent preparation for people who are willing to take that kind of risk. Another way to innovate is to design changes with balance in mind.

In "Goldilocks and the Three Bears," Goldilocks seeks balance by pursuing the principle of "Just Right." She is guided by this principle when she rejects the porridge that is too hot and too cold, the chair that is too big and too little, and the bed that is too soft and too hard. This search for the "middle way," when applied with the spirit of Goldilocks, can add balance to our teaching and our lives. It is generally wise to avoid extremes because of their consequences. For example, if we are too easy, students may not respect us. If we are too hard, they can lose confidence and become discouraged. When we create balance between too easy and too hard, just the right amount of effort is called forth, so things work more smoothly.

Creative Spirit:
"Cultivate balance,
then watch wisdom grow."

Consult Your Inner Family

We are often of two minds about things. In fact, several voices within us may speak out when we consider trying more risky options. In teaching, one part of us may strongly encourage a more creative approach, another might offer warnings, while a third voice condemns the venture as "foolhardy." As you consider becoming a more creative teacher, various voices may carry on a loud squabble within you. One way to handle the conflict is to let one voice dominate the outcome, but another part of you might feel guilty, afraid, or annoyed. Another approach is to take the middle way by encouraging the members of your inner family to compromise so all feel satisfied enough to embrace the change. This compromise makes gradual innovations in teaching possible.

Individual Process (30 minutes): Spend a few minutes noting the reactions of key members of your inner family to the prospect of becoming a more creative teacher. Become aware of their perspectives, yearnings, and interests. Notice the conflicts between them.

Identify a major change that your most creative side would encourage

With your eyes closed, consult the members of your inner family who have a stake in the situation. Ask them how they feel about the change. If they are reluctant, what modifications would they suggest in the plan so they could support it?

When you open your eyes, make appropriate notes. Use what you have written to revise the change in order to satisfy the interested parties. With your eyes closed, check with them to make sure the revision is acceptable. If there is resistance, revise again.

When you achieve an acceptable compromise, briefly describe how the change in your teaching will be made. Be specific.

If you are working with a partner or group, discuss what you learned.

I have used most teaching and grading systems. I have lectured, emphasized discussion, used experiential exercises, and allowed students to run courses. I used multiple choice exams, essay tests, take-home exams, and let students evaluate and grade themselves. When I chose a highly conventional or radical extreme, I experienced an inner rebellion. When I lectured in a conventional way, a part of me cried out, "Can't you teach in a more creative way?" When I was too permissive, a condemning voice whispered "Shame on you for failing to do your duty."

Making an abrupt change or choosing a balanced approach are options. What choice you make will depend on the teaching challenge you want or can tolerate. As Jane Thompson discovered, all innovations become learning experiences, even when they make us feel guilty and afraid.

Creative Spirit:
*"Balance has the magical capacity
to make things work better with less effort."*

"Too" Is A Balancing Word

Many teachers fail to use balance as a standard for guiding their decisions, which is why workloads often become too heavy. Requiring too little effort can also be a problem. By focusing on "too much" and "too little," we create reasonable workloads for ourselves and our students.

Creative Spirit:
*"Give yourself and your students a break!
Make work loads light enough so all of you
can maintain a little smile while carrying them."*

Individual Process (20 minutes): Your workload: Divide a journal page in half. On one half, note instances where you are doing too much work. On the other, note examples where you might benefit from working harder.

Reflect on your discoveries. How balanced is your work-load? If it is out of balance, what could be reduced or omitted entirely? What might be significant to add? Record your choices.

If you are working with a partner or group, share your insights.

Individual Process (20 minutes): The workload that you require of your students: Divide a journal page in half. On one half, record what you are asking students to do that may be "too much." On the other, note what may be "too little."

Reflect on your discoveries. How balanced is the workload you require of your students? If it seems unbalanced, what changes could you make? What could you reduce or cut out? What might you add? Note your decisions.

If you are working with a partner or group, share your insights and choices.

New teachers, but also those who are messianic about their teaching missions, may require too much of themselves and their students. Instead of providing time for thinking and reflection, education becomes a heavy burden of tasks that pushes everyone to the breaking point. As a graduate student doing research on education told me: "Education is about people making trouble for each other." When education becomes trouble for everyone, it loses its importance and vitality.

Using balance as a standard for teaching provides opportunities to make new choices. During a teaching workshop I led, a seasoned teacher commented, "I often feel frustrated because there is too much to cover in my introductory course. There never seems to be enough time to reflect. I rush from one topic to another, hoping students retain something of the mass of information I cover."

"Why do you teach that way?" I asked.

"I feel that I'm expected to" was her response.

"What if you just declared the right to choose for yourself? What would you do to create more balance?"

"Instead of trying to cover every topic in my field, I'd focus on key issues and take the time to go deeply into them. I'd encourage students to understand the issues in their complexity, so they would learn to think about them in new ways."

"Now that you know what you want to do, give yourself permission to do it."

"You mean I don't have to pack everything in? I can focus on what is truly important? I can decide?"

This teacher, who was widely respected for her impressive abilities, realized that she had the power to do things differently. In her moment of realization, I could see a little spark of freedom in her eyes.

Imagine dreaming that you are standing in front of a huge banquet table loaded with an amazing variety of foods. A voice says, "You must eat and digest everything you see." At what point would you become revolted by eating? Would you remember what you had eaten afterwards? Students sometimes experience their education in this way. Some classes become banquets of information that they are unable to fully consume or digest. It is little wonder that so many students lose their initial excitement for learning.

Creative Spirit:
"Don't be in a hurry to cover everything.
'Uncover' something.
Take a good look, a big listen,
a joyous, liberating breath.
Everybody's trying to figure it out."

Making More Time For Reflection

There is another imbalance in teaching. We pack so much material into our sessions that there is almost no time for reflection. How could reflection time be added to education so ideas can be quietly contemplated?

Individual Process (15 minutes): Divide a journal page into quarters. In three of them, sketch out ideas for types of reflection you might use in teaching. For example, "Deeper Thinking" would give students a few minutes to carefully contemplate an issue at depth.

In the fourth section, create an unusual reflection technique and a catchy name.

Consider how you might incorporate these reflection techniques into your teaching. How and when would you use them?

If you are working with a partner or group, share what you

invented.

Reflection time produces impressive results. It teaches students to dig more deeply into issues, to notice where they lack information, to discover their areas of confusion, and to think up new ideas and questions. It awakens their minds and draws them into the heart of learning. It also provides an opportunity for quieter students to collect their thoughts so they are better prepared to share and discuss their ideas. In general, reflection will improve the quality and depth of any discussion, because students will have the time to think before they speak.

Creative Spirit:
"Contemplation is incubation.
Use reflection time to nurture
new ideas and discoveries.

Creative Side Trip

Consulting Goldilocks
about your teaching

Goldilocks represents the principles of balance and wisdom. If she were your teaching consultant, what would she say about the following issues in your teaching? Note her cryptic quotes of wisdom.

What wisdom would she offer about how to make your approach to teaching more creative?

```
Goldilocks says:



```

What wise statement would she make about how to manage fears that inhibit your creativity?

```
Goldilocks says:



```

What simple wisdom would she convey about how to increase your enjoyment of teaching?

```
Goldilocks says:



```

Chapter 14

Stop The Stories
That Torture You

$\mathcal{H}$uman beings make up stories about almost everything. Embedded in our stories are beliefs about what is and what should be. A belief is a thought that we consider true or morally proper. Since beliefs develop slowly over time, we lose awareness of them and their influence, yet they limit our creativity as teachers and strongly affect our moods. When their influence is known, we can create a greater sense of personal contentment and freedom. When we learn to shape our stories, they stop limiting and torturing us.

Creative Spirit:
"Be aware of the beliefs you hold
as knots that restrict your thinking.
Which ones could be loosened or undone?"

Assumptions Are Limiting

Beliefs can become guiding assumptions that we never question. Those assumptions limit what we can perceive as options in teaching. By questioning our assumptions, we escape the limitations. With greater freedom to explore, we are able to consider creative ideas and approaches that our assumptions led us to exclude as possibilities.

Individual Process (30 minutes): Divide a journal page in half.

In one part, identify assumptions you hold about yourself as a teacher. These will be the beliefs you take for granted and never question.

In another, identify assumptions you hold about your students.

Circle the assumptions in each part that most restrict your creativity as a teacher.

In each half, identify your most limiting assumption.

Select one of those assumptions to "Run the Bases," a technique for generating four creative ideas about any issue.

Begin by drawing a baseball diamond with home plate and three bases in the corners. Write the assumption you selected in the center.

Start by crossing out the assumption. Experience the freedom of escaping your thinking restriction so you can invent new ideas for teaching.

Free from the limitation, run the bases.

When you get to first base, jot down a novel idea that you might use in teaching.

Go to second base. Dream up another creative possibility.

Go to third. Invent a riskier idea.

As you move toward home plate, dream up a surprising possibility.

Circle your most promising idea. Briefly describe how you will incorporate it into your teaching.

If you are working with a partner or group, share what you learned and created.

Beliefs restrict our creativity as teachers. Unaware of how they limit our thinking, we become confined without knowing it. Those limitations may emerge from unquestioned assumptions that make up the "true" stories we tell about our abilities; others may be assumptions we hold about our students and their behavior. Think of the story we might tell if one of our students walks out of class without warning.

As the student leaves, a story is likely to emerge automatically about our teaching ability. "I must be boring" is a common belief that arises to torment us, which may undermine our confidence and capacity to teach for the rest of the period. By stopping those negative stories and just stating the facts, our ego size is preserved, so we are able to maintain our effectiveness. When a student leaves, stating the fact —"A student is leaving and I don't know why"— is all that is necessary. We are unaware of the student's reason for leaving, so why make up a damaging story about it? The student may be ill or have a medical appointment.

Janet described a difficult experience she had with a teacher when she needed to leave class early to keep a doctor's appointment. As she walked from her seat to the door, the teacher stopped his lecture and stared at her. Having created a negative story about her exit, he could not contain his feeling of disappointment, which took the form of a snide comment to her as she was about to leave. His humiliating remark made her feel so miserable that she was unable to return to her classes in the afternoon. Had this teacher simply acknowledged that a student was leaving without telling himself a negative story about it, he would have avoided feeling rejected and Janet would not have felt depressed for the rest of the day.

Ideals Can Torture Us

Ideals are beliefs about the way things should be, including "Students should not walk out of class early." What happens in any class period is measured against those ideals. When a session approximates an ideal, our feelings of happiness and fulfillment create "a good teaching day." When it falls far short, our disappointment may be so great that we fall into a troubling mood. If our ideals are lofty, they are more likely to torture us and make us feel miserable as teachers. By modifying our ideals with balance in mind, we can put a stop to the agony.

Individual Process (30 minutes): In your journal, note key ideals that you have about yourself as a teacher. Those are the "should be" statements that guide your teaching. For example, you may try to live up to the ideal "I should be inspiring."

Next, note ideals that you hold about how your students should think and behave. For example, "They should be prepared for class by doing their homework."

Looking over the ideals you hold about yourself, identify your most compelling one. Describe how you will feel when you fail to achieve it.

What is the most important ideal you hold about your students? Describe how you feel about them when they fail to live up to it.

For a few minutes, consider how your ideals make you suffer as a teacher. From that awareness, what new choices appear? Note them.

If you are working with a partner or group, share what you learned.

Creative Spirit:
*"For one day, suspend the ideals
that cause you the most suffering as a teacher.
What new possibilities open up in your teaching?"*

While ideals perform the important function of keeping our objectives clearly in mind, they may also have teeth that bite into us. Perfectionists are particularly prone to have ideals with sharp teeth. Their hopes and standards are so high that they suffer from many disappointments. While perfectionism has the positive advantage of making people work harder, it also causes a lot of anxiety and distress. If perfectionists could modify their ideals so they were not so lofty, they could still have clear objectives but suffer less. In seeking greater balance about your ideals, try applying the principle: "Not too high, not too low."

Individual Process (10 minutes): Among your ideals, identify two with the sharpest teeth. Modify them to reduce the severity of their bite, using the principle of "Not too high, not too low." For example, the ideal "I must know the answers" might become "I will strive to be informed, but when I don't know the answer to a question, I'll admit it, then I'll get the information I need and report back."

Examining your modified ideals, what changes become possible in your teaching?

If you are working with a partner or group, share your discoveries.

One way to minimize our disappointments as teachers is to quickly notice the ideals behind them, then modify the ideals so their bite is not so painful. The other alternative is to continue pursuing high ideals and consciously embrace the suffering they cause.

What is the wise course for you?

Sharper Focus: For a few minutes, examine the nature of beliefs. What are they? Why do they have such power over you? How will you get some power over them?

Instead of being subservient to your beliefs, begin to master them. Knowing they are just thoughts, shape them to your purposes.

Creative Spirit:
"If you want to have fun, scare your thoughts
by becoming more aware of them.
They know that your awareness
is the greatest threat to their domination."

Chapter 15

Give Up Resistance
And Resignation

*G*rading student work is required, but many of us resist our role as evaluators. We oppose what we cannot change and suffer from it. Students suffer from their own forms of resistance. As final exams approach, I ask my students how many are resisting them. Everyone's hand goes up. "How many of you can get rid of finals?" No hands are raised. "So, what's your choice?" Silence usually falls over the group until eventually someone will say, "We can resist them and make ourselves miserable or we can accept them as something we can't change and stop our suffering." When a situation cannot be changed by our efforts, no resistance is the wise path. When we manage our thinking, we reduce our suffering.

In teaching, as in life, we carry a mental file cabinet full of templates for every situation. A template is a pattern of expectations and desires for evaluating our circumstances. Ideals shape many of our templates, but not all of them. Remember the last time you were stuck in traffic. Did you become frustrated and annoyed? These reactions arise from the template "There shouldn't be traffic jams." Using that template, we resist traffic jams and suffer.

Giving Up Resistance

Our teaching templates can make us unhappy if we are unaware of their influence. When reality appears in violation of an expectation or desire, resistance is automatic. By banging our heads against reality, we achieve a headache by the end of the day. As soon as we give up resistance to what we cannot change, a new possibility appears that our resistance made it impossible for us to see. For example, when we quit resisting having to evaluate students' work, we may see the possibility of ending a pattern of procrastination around grading that has been haunting us for years.

Individual Process (20 minutes): What do you resist as a teacher that you know you cannot change? Jot down your ideas on a journal page.

Circle any example of resistance where the resulting suffering is significant.

Next to each item you circled, note how you will give up resisting it.

As you give up your resistance, what new possibilities in teaching appear? Note them.

If you are working with a partner or group, share what you learned.

Creative Spirit:
"For one day, teach without resistance.
With flexibility of mind, adapt to your circumstances."

When we struggle against circumstances beyond our control, our complaints produce resentments that undermine our enthusiasm and effectiveness as teachers. By giving up resistance and complaints, we become more flexible and adaptable, ready to respond creatively to what life serves up.

Lao Tzu
"Softness triumphs over hardness,
feebleness over strength.
What is more malleable is always superior
over that which is immoveable.
This is the principle of controlling things
by going along with them,
of mastery through adaptation."

Giving Up Resignation

There are things that annoy us that we can change. If resignation develops, our power to act may be temporarily suspended. To reactivate that power, notice where you have become resigned, then develop a clear commitment to make a change.

Individual Process (20 minutes): In teaching, what have you become resigned to that you could change with effort? Note your ideas on a journal page.

Circle any item where giving up resignation and undertaking a change could improve your effectiveness, enthusiasm, or satisfaction.

Develop a simple plan for making one of those changes.

- What do you want to change?
- What steps will you take to produce the change?
- What action will you take this week or today?

If you are working with a partner or group, share your plans.

Cultivation: With your eyes closed, consider the personal resources you will cultivate to quit resisting what you cannot change and how you will take action, instead of being resigned, when change is possible.

Instead of resisting what cannot be changed or living in resignation, imagine practicing the principle: "Change what I can change. Quit resisting and complaining about what I can't." How would your life as a teacher be altered if you adopted this simple principle?

Creative Spirit:
"A mind that can laugh at its own folly is wise.
Stopping the folly is even wiser."

Chapter 16

Use Questions To
Guide The Mind

*A*s teachers, we ask questions all the time. But, do we fully understand the importance of asking them? Take a moment to consider the following question.

What small change in your approach to teaching would make it more rewarding for you?

Notice what is occurring in your thinking as you contemplate the question. Your mind is automatically seeking an answer. The mind is obedient. In most cases, it does what it is told to do. When a question asks for options, it creates them. If you ask it a factual question, it will try to recall the appropriate fact. If you ask it to be wise about an issue, it will try to express wisdom. The activity of the mind is shaped by the kinds of questions we ask it to consider. When we become conscious of the power of our questions, they become important tools of exploration and change in teaching.

The Socratic Method of teaching is based on the ability to ask questions that deepen and expand any inquiry. Another approach which accomplishes that end and also causes forward momentum and change is "Strategic Questioning," developed by Fran Peavey in *By Life's Grace*. Whether we are guiding a classroom discussion or talking to a student about a personal matter, knowing how to ask strategic questions is a valuable skill. Peavey's ideas about strategic questioning are briefly summarized below, followed by opportunities for practice.

■ A strategic question avoids "Why?"

"Why aren't you doing your homework assignments?" In frustration, many teachers resort to this question without thinking. In contrast, strategic questioning avoids "why" questions. Instead, it emphasizes "how," "what," "where," and "when" questions because they create forward motion and expand options. "What are two changes you could make in your thinking or routine so you could get your assignments done on time?" This strategic question will make students think about what they could do differently, which is likely to produce better results than a condemning "why" question.

Individual Process (5 minutes): Take a few "why" questions you ask your students and convert them into "how," "what," "where" or "when" questions.

■ A strategic question creates motion.

A strategic question helps people move into action and make change. We could ask an unmotivated student: "What is one thing you could do that would increase your motivation?" If prejudice is your topic: "How could people reduce their prejudices toward others?"

Individual Process (5 minutes): Jot down a few strategic questions you could ask your students that would encourage forward motion.

Creative Spirit:
"Think of questions as the seeds of change.
What changes will your questions grow?"

■ A strategic question creates options.

Instead of asking a question with only one answer in mind, encourage the cultivation of options. By asking the mind to seek alternatives, thinking quickly expands to include new choices. The unmotivated student could be asked: "What are two or three changes you could make that would increase your motivation?" About prejudice: "What are three or four ways prejudice could be reduced?"

Individual Process (5 minutes): Identify a problem you would like your students to explore. Record a few strategic questions that would make them more aware of optional approaches or solutions to it.

Creative Spirit:
"Ask questions that cultivate new pathways
instead of deepening well-trodden ones."

■ A strategic question digs deeper.

When students are thinking on the surface of an issue, a strategic question will deepen their inquiry. "What more could you say about that idea?" "How would you take that idea to a deeper level?" These strategic questions encourage more careful and complex thinking on the part of students, so their fascination and understanding grow.

Individual Process (5 minutes): Note a few strategic questions you could use in your teaching to deepen the thinking of your students.

Creative Spirit:
"Use questions as digging tools."

■ A strategic question avoids "Yes" or "No" answers.

"Yes" and "no" questions do not give the mind enough to do. Compare the level and complexity of thinking required by the "yes/no" question, "Do you believe in equality?" versus the strategic question, "What are your views about equality?"

Individual Process (5 minutes): Take a few "yes/no" questions you might ask your students and convert them into strategic questions.

Creative Spirit:
"When you ask a simple 'yes/no' question,
your students will give a simple 'yes/no' answer.
Give their minds something more challenging to do."

■ A strategic question is empowering.

Questions that make students aware of concrete changes they could make empower them for action. "What are different ways you could become more creative in your work? What is one step that you could take this week?" Asking questions that empower students to change encourages their development.

Individual Process (5 minutes): Create a few strategic questions you could ask your students that would empower them to make changes.

Creative Spirit:
"Ask questions with growth in mind."

■ A strategic question asks the unaskable.

What are unaskable questions? The questions people avoid because they are afraid of the answers or because the questions are "politically incorrect."

Individual Process (5 minutes): Take an important issue you will cover in your teaching. Ask two or three unaskable questions about it.

Creative Spirit:
*"When you dig up what's hidden,
you may discover a treasure."*

If you are working with a partner or group, share what you learned about the importance of questions.

Deeper Thinking: With your eyes closed, become more aware of how you will use questions with greater clarity and purpose in your teaching.

Imagine teaching a class with the talent for asking questions that significantly shapes the activity of the mind.

What did you do to become so effective at asking questions?

What personal resources did you draw upon?

What new gifts did you cultivate to sharpen your skill?

Chapter 17

Listening Deeply

$\mathcal{K}$nowing how to listen deeply is important for leading discussions and responding effectively to problems that students bring to us on a regular basis. As we listen, it is relatively easy to hear what students say about the facts of a situation and their feelings, but there are deeper levels we often miss that could increase our understanding and compassion. Deep listening helps us to hear and acknowledge more of the student. To practice listening at that depth, invite another person to be your partner or, if you want to work in a larger group, ask four others to join you.

Epictetus
"We have two ears and one mouth
so that we can listen twice as much as we speak."

Opening Process for Partners and a Group (15 minutes): As preparation for working with a partner or group, write about an issue that is important to you. It might be a social issue, a concern about teaching, or a transition you are going through. Allow the writing to occur spontaneously and quickly. Do not worry about the form; just capture the substance. When your writing is finished, read on.

There are four things to listen for when another person is speaking.

■ Facts

A person's description of the facts offers an overview of an issue or situation. Listening for the facts establishes an understanding of the person's interpretation of circumstances and events.

■ Feelings

Feelings convey the emotional tones of an issue or situation. Even when feelings are held back, they will be noticeable in the background. Listening for them provides an understanding of the person's emotional connection to the issue or situation.

■ Needs

Personal needs are seldom communicated directly, but can be heard between the lines. By consciously listening for needs, they become obvious. Needs affect feelings and the interpretation of facts, so their influence is more profound. When a person's needs are heard, a deeper part of the person is known.

■ Desired outcomes

A subtle aspect of any communication are the outcomes a person desires. These are the changes the person wants or hopes will occur. When someone is speaking about social issues, the desired changes may be obvious, but, in many other cases, they may be obscure. When desired outcomes are not openly declared, listen carefully to determine what they are. When you know a person's desired outcomes, you become aware of their hopes for change.

Process for Partners (35 minutes): Begin by dividing a page into four sections. Label them "Facts," "Feelings," "Needs," and "Desired Outcomes." Decide who will speak and who will listen during the first round.

How the process works: Using what was written earlier, the speaker shares his or her story. As the story is being told, the partner listens for facts, feelings, needs, and desired outcomes, briefly taking notes within the appropriate sections of the page. When the speaker is finished, the listener may spend a few minutes asking questions to fill in what may have been missed or not completely covered. For example, "Among your needs, which ones most directly influence your orientation to this issue?"

When the person listening has collected enough information at each of the four levels, feedback is given to the speaker in the following order: Facts, feelings, needs, and desired outcomes. Do not try to fix anything. Just convey what you heard.

Switch partners and repeat the process.

At the end, share your discoveries.

Creative Spirit:
"What if listening deeply was as necessary
as a morning's caffeine jolt."

Process for a Group (50 minutes): Five people are required

for this group exercise. Adjust the assignment of roles during the exercise if there are more or less than five. If the
number is greater than five, more than one person can take
the same role in each round. If less, one person can take
two roles in each round.

Select a facilitator who will keep the process moving so
everyone has a chance to share and be heard. Sit in a circle.
Assign a letter from A through E around the circle in a
clock-wise sequence.

Following are the roles and the rotations for the five rounds.

Roles:

0=storyteller
1=facts
2=feelings
3=needs
4=desired outcomes

Rotations:

	A	B	C	D	E	(group members)
Round 1:	0	1	2	3	4	
Round 2:	4	0	1	2	3	
Round 3:	3	4	0	1	2	
Round 4:	2	3	4	0	1	
Round 5:	1	2	3	4	0	

In the first round:

"A" tells the story.

"B" listens for and writes down what was heard about the facts of the situation.

"C" listens for and notes what was heard about feelings.

"D" listens for and records what was heard about needs.

"E" listens for and makes notes about desired outcomes.

After the story is finished, make your way around the circle: "B" shares what was heard about the facts, "C" about feelings, "D" about needs, and "E" about the desired outcomes.

Make the feedback simple, clear, and to the point. Keep the rotations moving. This is a gentle reminder for the extroverts who will want to give their account of the issue when they should be listening. Avoid a discussion of the issues. Just listen to the story, give feedback, then proceed to the next round.

After everyone's story has been heard, each person can briefly share insights that arose from the feedback. After members of the group have completed that sharing, others can offer their perspectives about the issues, if there is time.

Creative Spirit:
"Teach class by not talking so much.
Imagine that the fate of humanity depends on
listening to what students have to say today."

While objective thinking in education is widely encouraged, students will still have feelings, needs, and desires for change. So will you. By listening deeply, more of the richness of human communication is heard and brought into teaching. This ability to listen with a sensitive ear can be used during discussions or when you are helping students with thier personal problems. By listening to your students deeply, you will hear and understand them more completely. When you convey what you have heard to them, they will develop a clearer understanding of themselves.

Creative Side Trip

Listen in order to learn

If you listened to your students deeply for one week, what might you learn about them and from them that you are failing to fully perceive now?

I might learn:

I might learn:

I might learn:

Chapter 18

Leading Dynamic Discussions

To share, talk about, dig deeply into, debate, be moved and changed by: These descriptions capture the potential of discussions when people can freely communicate their ideas to each other. Discussion has an important purpose in education when it is used to deepen understanding of an issue through free self expression.

How can freedom of expression be cultivated?

What questions will enrich and expand any discussion?

How can listening deeply transform discussions into a vital part of the learning process?

Creative Spirit:
"Discussions are gardening opportunities.
How will you dig, plant, and nourish so
you get some blossoms?"

Preparing For Discussion

Carefully laying the groundwork for a discussion increases the chances that it will be dynamic and effective. Four issues are important: Social connection, security, interest, and giving students something to share.

Individual Process (20 minutes): Identify a topic you will teach where you would like to use discussion as your teaching tool. Note the issue at the top of a journal page.

■ Create social connection

Students will participate more openly in discussions when they feel socially connected to each other. For example, this might be achieved by arranging the chairs in the room in such a way that it is easier for them to see and speak with each other.

In your journal, briefly note two ways you could set up the seating arrangement before a discussion that would create good social connections between students. Make one of your ideas unorthodox.

■ Create security

When students are afraid, their dominant strategy will be to hold back. For them to feel free to share, they must feel safe. Identify at least two practices you will use during discussions that will make students feel safe to participate.

■ Create interest

If students are not interested in a topic or how it is presented, they will be reticent to participate in a discussion of the issues.

Note at least two ways you can make your topic interesting.

What interesting question or story could you use to open the discussion? Note one.

■ Create an experience so students have something to share

To increase the chances of full participation during a discussion, create an opening experience that gives students something to contribute. Put something in their minds before starting the discussion. For example, you could ask them to write down a novel question that they would want addressed during the discussion. If you are going to discuss a problem, you could ask them to close their eyes and imagine how the future would look if the problem were solved.

Record two ideas for simple opening exercises that would give your students something to share during the discussion. Take your most promising idea and sketch out the exercise.

If you are working with a partner or group, share how you will create social connection, security, interest, and an experience for your students.

Creative Spirit:
"How can you make your students
comfortable challenging your ideas?
How can you make yourself comfortable
receiving those challenges?"

Leading The Discussion

During the discussion, use listening skills and questions to deepen and expand the inquiry. The deeper the discussion goes, the more interesting the issue becomes. The more students are interested in the issue, the more they will learn. Think depth, then create it in the way you ask questions, listen, dig deeper, contribute, and invite students to share their ideas and experiences.

Individual Process (20 minutes): On a journal page, put "Questions that will deepen the discussion." Staying with the topic above, note a few questions that would deepen the exploration of its many facets during a discussion.

Add strategic questions that might expand awareness of options and encourage changes in understanding, attitudes, and behavior.

Circle your most promising questions.

Choose two that seem crucial and ask a couple of probing questions about them that will expand or deepen thinking about the issue.

If you are working with a partner or group, share your questions.

Since the objective of a discussion is to create depth of understanding, a good teacher will not be content with a level of inquiry if it can be taken deeper. Asking questions is the tool to deepen it.

Other questions to consider while guiding a discussion.

■ What most challenges us about this problem?

- How do we contribute to it?
- How do we feel about it?
- How does it affect our needs?
- What parts of the problem are we failing to see?
- What parts are we consciously avoiding?
- What would be an unpopular approach to this issue?
- What are our most important ideas so far?
- How are those ideas connected?
- Which connections should we explore more deeply?
- What have we learned so far?
- What other perspectives should we consider?
- What would be a surprising question to ask now?
- What are possible solutions to the problem?
- Which would be the most creative solution?
- How will we determine the best solution?
- What would "best" mean?
- What negative results might each solution create?
- What change would we personally like to see?
- How would we contribute to the change?

Creative Spirit:
"Use props in class this week to stimulate discussion.
How will it change the tone of the class?
How will it change your attitude?"

Quiet And Talkative Students

Every classroom full of students is a random collection of unique psychological types. This makes teaching interesting, but also a challenge. At times, fate will give us a sizeable number of introverts, so leading a good discussion and encouraging participation become more difficult. Some of our students may be extreme extroverts who will naturally want to dominate discussions. When the extremes of type are present, difficulties may arise during discussions that fail to appear in classes where the extremes are not so great.

Individual Process (10 minutes): Imagine being a quiet student in one of your classes. Experience the reluctance to speak during a discussion because you want to avoid being in the spotlight or to divulge your views in public. You may be happy with your quiet nature, but feel vulnerable when there is pressure to participate. You may notice your energy draining away during the day as teacher after teacher encourages you to participate. Your proving ground is not participation, but in activities you do alone, where you have time to reflect and perform at your best. Being that quiet person, consider your responses to the following questions.

■ How do you want to be treated by the teacher?
■ What would make you feel safer during discussions?
■ What would make you want to contribute?
■ What would lead you to participate, even when afraid?

If you are working with a partner or group, share what your introverted student taught you about how to treat quiet people and encourage their participation during discussions.

Honoring the nature of quiet students is an important part of respect. Unfortunately, when participation is graded, they are punished for their introversion. While they may be reluctant to share their ideas, introverted students may be engaged in thinking about the issues, often at considerable depth. They feel safer working in small groups and most comfortable sharing ideas with a partner. When leading a discussion, starting with partners talking gives introverts a chance to think, so when the large group discussion starts, they have something already formulated in their minds. This increases the chances that they will contribute.

Creative Spirit:
"When quiet students aren't speaking, realize that their minds may be having a meaningful conversation."

Without extroverts, discussions would fall flat. They keep the exchange lively and engaging. On occasion, extroverts may dominate a discussion, which can make the less talkative students feel excluded. How to handle the extreme extrovert is part of the challenge of facilitating an effective discussion.

Individual Process (10 minutes): Imagine being an extroverted student in one of your classes who loves to talk and, caught up in the excitement of participation, tends to dominate discussions. Feel the need to have the spotlight on you and your ideas. Notice how you gain energy from social interaction, so discussion feeds you. When you participate, the time flies and, if your contributions are well received, you leave the classroom feeling good. Discussions are your proving ground. Being that talkative student, respond to the following questions.

- How do you want to be treated by the teacher?
- What makes you want to contribute so often?
- How could you encourage other students to share?
- What could a teacher say that would stop you from dominating the discussion but would not feel like a harsh criticism?
- When and where would you want the teacher to raise that issue with you?

If you are working with a partner or group, share what your extroverted student taught you about how to treat talkative students and how to quiet down extreme talkers.

Creative Spirit:
*"When students can't stop talking,
be infected by their enthusiasm,
then create some of your own."*

Being aware of the nature of quiet and talkative students is important. For greater understanding of these and other issues, take the psychological type test and read about the various types in David Keirsey, *Please Understand Me II* or use his web site [http://Keirsey.com/]. As a teacher, it is important to know the psychological type that you are. It will help explain why you teach as you do. It will also reveal why some students annoy you while others seem wonderful. Knowledge of psychological types and human behavior will enrich your teaching in surprising ways.

A juggler learns to keep six balls in the air by practice. Teachers become effective discussion leaders in the same way. Creativity, understanding, and practice transform abilities to the point where the dynamics of discussion are mastered, so leading a discussion looks easy. But, like a juggler, full attention is still required.

Chapter 19

Be Receptive To Coaching

*O*ne semester I received a biting three page, single-spaced, anonymous letter from a student. It was full of resentment, misunderstanding, and criticism. It was a poisonous letter and it hurt me to read it. My ego felt deflated. I decided to set the letter aside and reread it when I felt greater inner strength. Two weeks passed before I was able to go back to it. I went through the letter carefully, underlining key points the student had made. I explored each criticism as a suggestion for change. Criticisms based on misunderstanding were discarded. Others revealed important ideas I needed to seriously address. Responding to those useful points, I made major changes in the course and the way I taught it. The ultimate result was that my teaching became more effective and the course grew into a more powerful learning experience for my students.

When we receive a criticism from a student or colleague about our teaching, what is our response? Do we listen attentively, trying to determine what might be useful among the suggestions we are hearing? Or do we become hurt, annoyed, angry, or defensive? Most people would agree that it is easier to give than get criticism. It does not have to be that way.

Individual Process (10 minutes): Take a few minutes to describe how you typically react when a student or colleague criticizes you and your teaching. What is your automatic emotional response?

Given your response, what story do you make up about the person and the situation?

How does that story affect how you listen?

Now that you are aware of the way you normally react, move into choice and change.

Note in a few sentences how you would listen if you interpreted "criticisms" as "coaching."

Briefly describe how you would listen if, instead of thinking of the criticism as pointing out a "failure," you thought of it as "feedback."

Note how you would listen if you interpreted the person's communication as a "gift" to help you improve what you are doing, not a "gripe."

Describe how you would listen if you interpreted what was said to you as that person's "perspective," not the "truth."

If you are working with a partner or group, share what you discovered.

A Shrinking Ego Fails To Listen

"Criticisms" have the effect of reducing the size of our egos. Feeling little, most of us are likely to automatically interpret and respond to criticism as an "attack," "personal failure," or "gripe." Unless we trust the critic to act in our interests, most of us become defensive, counterattack, or leave the scene as quickly as possible. Resistant to coaching, we lose access to ideas that might have had a positive impact on our teaching.

We develop an aversion to criticism about our teaching because it deflates our egos, which accentuates our feelings of inadequacy. Once the automatic nature of our response is understood, we are able to stop the ego from deflating by establishing a Recovery Claim to manage our ego size so we can listen and learn. "I'm good enough" or "I'm strong enough to listen and learn from this" are claims that can make us more receptive listeners. Through that openness, we become the beneficiaries of new information.

Creative Spirit:
"When you close your ears,
you also close your mind."

When we resist criticisms about our teaching in order to preserve the size of our egos, we involuntarily reject the feedback without carefully weighing its benefits. This is especially the case when the criticism makes us feel little, because we are apt to discount the idea in order to continue feeling big. "No, that is not a better idea" may be our knee-jerk reaction when someone suggests a change in our teaching. We make up our minds so quickly out of self-defense that we fail to seriously consider what is being said. Becoming open to coaching is an alternative way of responding to "criticism," so we get maximum value from it. The ordinary way that people respond to criticism is defense, counterattack, or flight. The extraordinary way is to be coachable, which is the capacity to listen in a state of readiness to learn and change.

To become more receptive to coaching, change your story by altering your interpretation of the situation.

■ Instead of thinking "criticism," say "coaching."

■ Instead of interpreting what is being said as a personal "failure," call it "feedback."

■ Instead of thinking "gripe," embrace the feedback as a "gift" to improve your efforts.

■ Instead of interpreting what the person says as the "truth," see it as a "perspective."

Individual Process (5 minutes): Close your eyes. Imagine receiving a criticism from a student or colleague. Perhaps it is a complaint you already received but were not willing to hear. In that situation, imagine yourself thinking "coaching," "feedback," "gift," and "perspective" while the "complaint" is being offered. See yourself being receptive to the coaching. Notice what you learn.

If you are working with a partner or group, share what you saw and what you will do to become more coachable.

Creative Spirit:
"Your capacity to learn increases as your capacity to listen increases."

Creativity is directly related to learning, change, and effectiveness. When we are receptive to coaching, our minds enter a state of heightened receptivity: "I'm listening and willing to learn." With that receptive listening, our creative potential expands because we are freer to receive and use suggestions for change. We are more able to incorporate the ideas, abilities, and understanding of others to increase our effectiveness. Continuous learning through this openness to feedback nourishes our creativity as teachers.

To the extent that we are receptive to coaching, we are more likely to get detailed feedback. If you have coached someone who responded defensively to your feedback, you probably failed to provide the depth or detail in your critique that you would have with someone who was a receptive listener. Coaches hold back details when the person being coached shows indifference or assumes a defensive or offensive stance. Therefore, only the vague outlines of key points are communicated. This weakens the coaching because it will lack depth and clarity.

Once you are receptive to coaching, you can:

■ Seek additional information

This is an opportunity to seek greater clarification and more specific details about the other person's ideas. "Could you say something more about . . ?" becomes a vital question in the repertoire of a creative person who is receiving feedback. By seeking clarification and additional information, the person being coached is in a better position to consider and evaluate suggestions.

■ Listen, but reserve judgment

It is unnecessary to make choices during a coaching session.

Just listen carefully and try to understand. Avoid the automatic reaction "Yes, you're right. I'll do that," unless the idea is definitely one you want to try. You can tell your coach that time is needed to evaluate the feedback. Most coaches will be so delighted with your openness that they will honor your right to ponder and weigh what has been recommended. If any changes are made, letting your coach know is a good idea, because it creates the conditions for future coaching from that person. Great mentoring emerges when the person being helped is fully open to coaching.

■ Seek positive feedback

There are few good coaches because most people focus only on what we need to change and omit any consideration of what we are doing well. If your coach is typical and focuses only on your shortcomings, seek positive feedback by asking for it. "What do you notice that I'm doing well?" Not only is positive feedback helpful for managing the size of our egos, it is important for learning what we are doing well, so we will keep doing it. When positive feedback is received, it makes us more receptive to coaching and it helps to clarify achievements for us and our coach. So ask for positive feedback if it is withheld. It adds balance to any coaching session.

If your ego begins shrinking during a coaching session, asking for positive feedback is helpful. So is the use of a Recovery Claim. If both fail to make you receptive, postpone the coaching. Postponement will give you a chance to change your interpretation of the situation so you are better prepared to listen and learn when the coaching resumes.

■ Seek coaching

When we are receptive to coaching, we can actively seek it.

"What people might help me improve my ability or enhance my knowledge? When will I ask for their help?"

Individual Process (15 minutes): Spend a few minutes thinking about people from whom you might want coaching. Identify their names in your journal and briefly note what you would like to learn from them. Circle your most promising possibility and then set a date when you will seek coaching from that person. Arrange the coaching session, then practice being receptive.

Steps To Becoming Coachable

Step one: When someone says something that seems like "criticism," think of it as coaching, feedback, a gift, and a useful perspective. Avoid slipping into a defensive or attack posture, but remain open and accepting. Realize that feedback is a point of view that might give you new information or perspectives.

Step two: Maintain your ego size by using a good Recovery Claim: "I can listen to and learn from this coaching because I know I'm a worthwhile person."

Step three: Once you establish ego size and receptivity, you will be in a better position to seek feedback in detail. Ask for clarification and more information. Do not judge what you are hearing, just fully hear it.

Step four: Know that you can postpone making a decision while you are being coached. The point is to listen for alternatives. Take some time to consider the ideas before making decisions about them.

Step five: If you fail to receive positive feedback, ask for it.

It will increase understanding of what you are doing well, which will reinforce it. This will make the coaching session more effective and you will end on a positive note.

Step six: Thank your coach and let her or him know that you will think about the coaching and make some decisions.

Step seven: If you decide to change something based on the coaching, let your coach know. This will increase the likelihood of additional coaching in the future.

Becoming receptive to coaching requires diligent practice in order to counter our automatic emotional reactions while receiving a critique.

How will you practice being receptive to coaching this week?

How will you actively seek coaching?

When you have learned to be receptive to coaching, you increase your chances of being an effective coach for others, which is the issue we address next. If you are working alone, seek a partner. Ask your partner to read and do the work in this chapter as preparation.

Chapter 20

Coach Effectively

Jn teaching, coaching is the active mentoring of students with their development and well-being in mind. Effective coaching combines suggestions for change with acknowledgments about what students are doing well. By balancing criticism and positive acknowledgments, the ego size of students is preserved, so they are able to listen more receptively to suggestions while maintaining enough confidence to sustain their creative momentum. To practice this balanced approach to coaching, you will need a partner. If you are working in a group, create pairs.

Creative Spirit:
"Like balloons, students' egos aren't tough
but they are susceptible to sudden collapses.
How will you coach so your students don't deflate?"

Individual Process (10 minutes): On a journal page, briefly describe your existing style of giving feedback to students. Be specific.

If you were receiving the kind of feedback you give, what impact would it have on your motivation and capacity to learn?

What specific effects do you think your style of giving feedback has on your students?

If effective coaching is the capacity to make students receptive to feedback, learning, and change, in what ways are you effective or ineffective as a coach?

Share what you learned with your partner.

Individual Process (50 minutes): Write a one to two page story about any topic. It could be a fictional encounter over coffee with a friend or perhaps you might enjoy writing a fairytale. Establish "courage" and "curiosity" as your inspiration points. Let your story develop spontaneously. Use your imagination and have fun! Take about 20 minutes for writing.

When your story is finished, exchange it with your partner, so the criticism phase can begin. After reading your partner's story, respond in writing to the following questions.

- What do you like about the work? Be specific.
- What would you change?

What might be omitted?

What could be elaborated upon?

What could be changed in the story to make it more interesting or compelling?

What might be added?

■ What else do you like about the work? Be specific.

Notice that these questions are arranged like a sandwich: Positive acknowledgments on the top and bottom, suggestions as filling in the middle. This approach to evaluation is used in Toastmasters International, an organization which provides opportunities for becoming a more effective public speaker. It is called the "Sandwich Technique."

When you have completed your written critiques, decide who will be coached first. Switch roles after the first round. As you are being coached, keep an open attitude and strive to be receptive rather than defensive. While coaching, move through the following steps.

Step one: Ask the person if he or she would like your coaching and feedback. Let the person know that you are offering the coaching to improve results. Show that you care for the person's well-being and success.

Step two: If the response is positive, tell the person that you are offering your viewpoint and it is up to him or her to evaluate it and determine what might be useful.

Step three: Use the "Sandwich Technique" when giving feedback.

Examine what you wrote about your partner's story. Notice that it is organized as a coaching sandwich. Use it to offer feedback in the following way:

First Slice of bread: Provide positive feedback. What is the person doing well?
The meat or veggies: These are your suggestions for change. Offer them as simply and clearly as possible.

Second slice of bread: End with more positive feedback. What else has the person done well?

Step four: Thank the person being coached for listening, then offer to be coached, so that coaching is established as something everyone needs.

Creative Spirit:
"If the filling of your coaching sandwich is hefty, increase the thickness of the bread."

Start the coaching process. For the person being coached: If you feel your ego deflating during the coaching, state a Recovery Claim to yourself so you can listen and be receptive to the feedback. Ask for clarification of points if there is confusion. Seek more information to practice wanting more feedback. Coach, while following the steps for effective coaching, feel yourself caring about your partner's well-being and effectiveness.

When you have completed being coached and coaching each other, take time to reflect together. What did you learn? How will you use the Sandwich Technique in your teaching? If you are working in a larger group, reconvene for sharing.

Many teachers see their coaching role in a one-sided way. They provide criticisms but withhold positive feedback, so students may feel a temporary collapse of their egos. In that state of diminished self-confidence, careful listening is apt to diminish along with motivation and momentum.

After missing one of my classes, a student confided in me that she had received such a scathing criticism from a teacher that she had to go home. She spent the day in bed, depressed about her ability and questioning her value as a person. Teachers who are such harsh critics routinely create these effects in students. They offer criticisms thinking they are for the good of the student, but these one-sided critiques do more harm than good. They also miss some of the truth, because they fail to acknowledge what the student is doing well. In contrast, the Sandwich Technique helps a teacher capture more of the truth, while it preserves the ego size of students so they are able to expand their knowledge and abilities. Through effective coaching, some may eventually surpass the teacher, which is what a good teacher wants.

Use the Sandwich Technique to assess yourself and your work. After learning how to use this balanced approach to coach students, a bright, young graduate student began using it to critique herself and her work. She was surprised by the results. "Usually, I would think only about my shortcomings, so my confidence would suffer. When I began to look for what I was doing well, not only was I able to acknowledge the positive, but it gave me the strength to tackle what I needed to improve and change. What a revelation!"

Creative Spirit:
"To maintain effectiveness,
notice what you are doing well
before looking at your shortcomings,
then end on a positive point."

Be Aware Of Your
Emotions While Coaching

Have you ever been coached by a person whose anger or disappointment was a strong undercurrent of the coaching? How did it affect the way you listened? Did you wonder why the person was so annoyed?

Individual Process (15 minutes): What emotions do you bring to coaching? Divide a journal page in half.

In one part, list the emotions you experience when, upon assessing a student's work, you are impressed with its quality.

How would expressing those positive feelings during a coaching session affect the student's willingness to listen and learn?

In the other part, note emotions that emerge when you feel critical of the quality of a student's work.

How would the undercurrent of those emotions affect a coaching session and the student's capacity to listen and learn?

What are you noticing about your emotions and coaching?

What new choices are possible?

Is there a new practice you would like to try?

Share your work with your partner. If you are working in a group, reconvene for sharing.

Emotions make their way into our evaluation of others. If

we are impressed with someone's work, we are likely to feel good and express it. When we are critical, we may feel disappointed and even angry. Without realizing it, we may believe that the person being coached made the errors just to irritate us, so our resentment is added to the feedback. During the coaching session, our anger may break out into the open if it is intense, although usually we will try to contain it. Even when we hide our hostility, the person being coached is apt to sense and react to it. Unaware that we have poisoned the coaching session with our hostility, we may be caught off guard when the person reacts with hurt feelings or anger, which is apt to annoy us all the more.

Offering suggestions and listening with a touch of compassion is what gives coaching its special power to cultivate growth and change. One aspect of compassion is the willingness to enter into the reality of others and to forgive them for being human. When we are coaching, it is knowing that people will make mistakes and they did not make them to annoy us. For the person being coached, it is knowing that a coach will have negative emotional reactions at times and to listen for the feedback in spite of them. By knowing that the pitfalls of being human are inescapable, we soften our judgments of each other so we can teach and learn together.

Creative Spirit:
"Instead of cutting down a person to stimulate growth,
try gentle pruning as a wiser approach."

Creative Side Trip

Avoid taking it personally

Many emotional upsets occur because we take what others say and do personally. What can you stop taking personally, so you feel more at ease as a teacher?

I will stop taking personally:

I will stop taking personally:

I will stop taking personally:

Chapter 21

"Nightmare" Students

$\mathscr{P}$arker Palmer writes about the power of "the student from hell" to disturb a teacher's tranquility in *The Courage To Teach*. Those are our nightmare students. Like nightmares during sleep, we wish they did not exist, but they do. The "unmotivated" may sit in the back of the room with no interest in learning. The "critics" may vigorously oppose our ideas at every turn. The "minimalists" may participate in class but do as little as possible of their assigned homework, avoid reading, miss deadlines, and then expect a high grade for minimal effort. "Tormentors" may have such high levels of hostility toward a teacher that they will engage in forms of ridicule in order to undermine the teacher's authority and confidence. If they constitute a group, their mission may be disruption for the sheer pleasure of it. "Tormentors" are the most nightmarish of students because they relish conflict. It gives them the spotlight and dominance. They become ego inflated by watching a teacher squirm or become angry. How to respond to these types of nightmare students is one of the creative challenges of teaching.

To understand nightmare students, consider their stories. The unmotivated live in stories about how they are burned out on school or how a particular subject holds no fascination for them. Critics exist in a story that education is about challenging the teacher's ideas. Minimalists tell themselves the story that they are doing a lot, even though reality indicates otherwise. Tormentors may have stories about how they are being harshly judged, picked on, or excluded by teachers. To try to change our nightmares, it is a good idea to first imagine the stories they are living within.

Individual Process (30minutes): On a journal page, identify the types of students that are your worst nightmares as a teacher.

Take your greatest nightmare. Describe what that student does that annoys you and makes teaching more difficult.

Describe your typical response to that student.

Now, imagine the story that nightmare student is living within. Briefly describe the story and how it might be shaping that student's attitude and behavior toward you, the class, and school.

With that understanding, note at least two new strategies for reaching that student with the objective of altering the student's story.

Select your most promising approach and develop it into a detailed strategy. Before developing your strategy, consider how you might include ideas from the following:

■ Your four ethical principles to guide what you say and do.

■ Deep listening of the student's story to cultivate understanding and relationship.

■ Strategic questions to create forward motion and change about the problem.

■ Receptivity to coaching so you can hear the student's

suggestions for change.

■ The "Sandwich Technique" to coach effectively.

Design your strategy. What exactly will you try? How will you reach the student to alter the student's story about you, the class, or education? How will your strategy help you to alter your story about the student?

Creative Expansion: Close your eyes and imagine yourself employing that strategy with other difficult students.

If you are working with a partner or group, share what you discovered and the new choices you made.

Having difficult students is not within our control, but how we respond to them is. Having a clear strategy in mind increases our capacity to act, which is the only way to alter a situation. Some of our efforts may fail, while others can succeed beyond our expectations.

Creative Spirit:
"Nightmares by night disappear by getting to know them. The same is true for Nightmare students by day."

Personal contact with nightmare students is probably our best chance of producing a change, because most of their stories have arisen as a result of their social distance from us. At a distance, they can make up all kinds of stories about us and what we are teaching. If they are part of a clique, a collective story will develop and be reinforced. Altering stories makes change possible–a student's story about us and our teaching and our story about the nightmare student. The "unmotivated" may respond positively to private meetings and special efforts to encourage their dreams and commitment. "Critics" may temper their criticisms if they get to know us better and we learn to use their criticisms constructively in class to deepen discussions. "Minimalists" may respond to strategic questions: "What changes could you make to increase your effort? How will learning to work harder now contribute to your success after graduation?" "Tormentors" may give up their active hostility when we speak to them in private about how their behavior is making us feel, by changing how we treat them, and by altering how we present the material of the class. By altering our stories about each other, there is an opportunity for change. If those efforts fail to produce good results and the student's behavior continues to be troublesome, seek advice and help from others. Staying isolated in the problem is not a good idea; seeking support is.

In classes that are more likely to trigger hostility because of their content, establishing four ethical ground rules with your students at the outset may be helpful. To the extent that students help to create the rules, they are more likely to live in harmony with them. Having simple and clear ground rules will increase your ability to respond to disruptive behavior when it occurs. If you are a woman who has tried everything and still experiences harassment from male students, explore Bernice Sandler's work called "The Chilly Classroom Climate." Her ideas and practical suggestions appear in *Women Faculty at Work in the Classroom, or Why It Still Hurts to be a Woman in Labor, The Chilly Classroom Climate: A Guide to Improve the Education of Women* (with Lisa Silverberg and Roberta Hall), and "How to Handle Disruptive Classroom Behavior" and "Intervening When Male Students Engage in Negative Behavior" under "The Chilly Climate" at her website: [www.bernicesandler.com].

Creative Spirit:
"Students are like roses.
Some may have thorns,
but they also have inner beauty,
if you take the time to look for it."

We Can Create Nightmare Students

When we are too rigid as teachers, we are likely to convert a few normal students into nightmares. If we become too pushy about our ideas, they may become hostile as a natural correction. When we are too flexible, they may become frustrated by our lack of guidance and complain about it. When we balance "rigid" and "flexible" in our approach, students are happier and teaching becomes easier.

Individual Process: (15 minutes): Divide a journal page in half. On one half, note examples where you are being too rigid or pushy as a teacher. It may be related to the structure of the class or issues. On the other half, record any instances where you are being so flexible that your students may feel that your guidelines are unclear.

Examine what you have written. Circle any item that is causing students to respond with resistance, complaint, or hostility. Taking your two most compelling cases, briefly describe how they are producing trouble in your teaching.

With that awareness, what will you change? Note your ideas.

Deeper probe: Recall how students relate to you when you are too rigid or pushy. How do they relate to you when you are too flexible? Imagine how they would respond if you were in better balance about rigid and flexible.

If you are working with a partner or group, discuss what you learned and will change.

Deep and honest personal engagement with sleeping nightmares is what makes them disappear. The same is true for the nightmare students who trouble you as a teacher. Just like sleeping nightmares, you may want to avoid them instead of reaching out to create rapport and understanding. Also, notice how you might be transforming normal students into nightmares by the way you teach. Knowing that being too rigid or being too flexible may work against you, choose to change what you are doing with balance in mind. By altering what you say and do that may be producing trouble, you reduce some of the burden of being a teacher. This can only make teaching easier and more rewarding.

Creative Spirit:
*"Instead of tightening the ropes until it hurts,
give yourself and your students some slack.
Notice how much easier teaching becomes
when the ropes are a bit loose."*

Chapter 22

Creativity Is Always Possible

*W*hen innovative teachers face circumstances that seem too limiting or too challenging for creativity to work, they may seek the safety of conventional methods of teaching. Some may set creativity aside when faced with educational requirements that are imposed from above, while others revert to a conventional style of lecturing when asked to teach a very large course. Yet, when "creative" is the first thing we say about ourselves as teachers, we know that creativity is always possible. I discovered this when I taught a 500-student introductory Sociology course.

When I first considered teaching the course, I thought "This is such a huge class, I'll probably have to lecture in the old way." It did not take me long to realize that, while this was the safer approach, lecturing from extensive notes again would be no fun for me, it might bore many of the students, and it would take the life out of my teaching. With those thoughts in mind, I decided to take the risk of teaching the course in an innovative way.

Creative Spirit:
"A bored mind is turned off.
Turn on the minds of your students,
then crank up the volume. Rock their worlds
by challenging them to think in new ways."

When I visited the lecture hall to check it out, I was amazed by its shabbiness. It had not been painted for years, tiles were dislodged from the ceiling, and the chairs were in need of repair or replacement. The acoustics were poor and the microphones and speaker system for projecting my voice were inadequate. Another major liability was a huge science experiment platform across the front of the room, so you had to navigate around it to get to the four large sliding chalk boards. The boards were the one feature of the room I liked.

Despite the dismal room, I wanted to discover whether it was possible to teach 500 students in a unique way. I ended up teaching the course for eight years. In the first year, I had the speaker system upgraded so students could hear me more easily. The next year, I had wireless microphones installed so students could share their ideas with each other. Each year, I created and tried new experiential learning processes and threw out what had not worked well the year before. The course soon became one of the most risky and dynamic learning experiences my students and I had ever undertaken. I still meet students from that class who fondly remember what we accomplished together. When you teach interactively, classes become mutual creations where everyone feels a sense of involvement and pride.

Creative Spirit:
"Work for illumination.
How will you help your students
see what they haven't seen yet?"

When I began designing the course, I wrote out my teaching objectives first. I realized that my main goal was to create a change in the way students thought about society. I wanted them to be able to think sociologically, so they could analyze social life in new ways and propose solutions to social problems. Key sociological concepts were identified as part of a thinking menu, which I used to sketch out the topics for each week.

With the weekly outline of the course completed, I created experiential exercises for each topic. Each exercise was developed with a clear commitment to engage students deeply in sociological concepts and issues, so they would be eager to share their experiences and ideas. I developed an interesting opening and closing for each class period. I imagined each session to be a pearl with its own beauty and integrity on a string of pearls, all fitting nicely together as a whole. I previewed films and videos, eventually selecting six that would stimulate thinking about an important concept or issue. I was interested in film as part of the variety that makes a course engaging to the mind. I invited a few interesting guest speakers for the same reason.

Since my main objective was to teach thinking skills, I created an evaluation strategy that relied heavily on writing assignments where students were challenged to think, understand, and explain. I chose one small textbook to provide an overview of the key concepts and issues and three engaging smaller books about specific social problems. Like the emphasis on writing, the choice of books was intended to stimulate and challenge students to think in new ways about social life and social change.

The day approached for me to teach the course for the first time. I was perspiring from anxiety as I prepared for the hour. Entering the room, I tried to appear calm. I put my teaching outline on the podium and began greeting students as they poured through the large doorways. When all the seats were taken, with dozens of students sitting in the aisles hoping to get in, I started the session. Imagine the feeling of looking up into a crowd of over 500 students who are waiting for you to inspire them.

Clear about my commitment to encourage active participation, I took students through an opening exercise that made them aware of their fears of participating and the personal resources they possessed to act in the face of fear. On my invitation, many wrote their fears and personal resources on the large chalk boards. Afterwards, they spoke about their fears, emphasizing what made them most reluctant to participate. They emphasized "feeling vulnerable," "being wrong," and "looking foolish" as leading fears. Among the personal resources they identified, "courage" was singled out as one they could all use. I asked them to raise their hands if they could use courage to participate in spite of their fears. Nearly everyone's hand went up. A commitment to participate had been established.

Each day afterwards, I guided students through learning processes that required their full involvement. When they held back, I asked them what resource they needed so they would be willing to take a risk. A student would shout "courage," then there would be an upsurge of risk-taking. Each day they accepted the challenge to participate. By taking risks, they did extraordinary things.

■ They debated and shared their ideas and discoveries with each other on hand-held microphones.

■ They took part in teaching demonstrations of fundamental principles in front of the class, for example, how social norms create patterns of conformity.

- They shared results from learning exercises by writing them on the large boards for all to see and for me to build upon.

- They volunteered to play roles in social dramas that provided important insights into issues and concepts.

- They used concepts from the thinking menu to analyze a social problem with a partner or in small groups, then shared their ideas with the class, either on the boards or on microphone.

- With their eyes closed, they imagined themselves in a variety of circumstances and brought back what they learned, then shared it.

- They participated in simulations that presented important principles of social dynamics, such as how and why enemies are created and how discrimination arises and is perpetuated.

- They carried out norm violations in class, which put them at risk of looking foolish.

- They shared personal experiences which revealed the impact of social problems on their lives.

- They engaged in meaningful discussions with each other about sensitive issues related to class, race, ethnicity, gender, and sexual orientation.

- They took the issues outside of the classroom by teaching others about them.

During the semester, a student would say to me: "This is an amazing learning experience. How is it possible that we're doing this together?" I usually responded with a question. "What makes you willing to participate and take risks so we can learn together?" "We seem to trust and support each other, so we're in this thing together." When we take the chance of teaching interactively, openness, trust, and the willingness to try are cultivated. Then, miracles become possible in education, even in a class of 500.

Creative Spirit:
"To create a miracle,
change what seems impossible
into a possibility."

While teaching this large class, I learned several important principles for increasing effectiveness in teaching.

■ Create a simple outline or flow diagram of the work you will do for each session. Make it easy to read, so a quick glance will reveal what to do next. Two pages of outline or diagram are usually sufficient for a 50 minute session.

■ Be ready to make modifications in your plan as you are teaching. You may have to remove less crucial parts of your design to complete a session. Be flexible enough to invent new exercises as you go along. Part of the fun of interactive teaching is the creativity that emerges during the process.

■ Prepare an interesting opening to each session and a compelling closing, when the important threads of the day's discoveries are pulled together. Engaging students' minds at the beginning and stimulating their thinking at the end is important for increasing the impact of ideas.

■ Make each session a unit, like a pearl on a strand of pearls. Trailing off at the end with "We'll finish this next time" fragments learning. Give each session its own integrity, then pace the work so you complete it.

■ Go to class ten minutes early. Spend that time talking to individuals or small groups of students. Ask them about changes they are noticing in their ability to think about and understand the issues.

■ Prepare quotes on sticky name tags that address important issues in the class. Before class, ask a few students if they are willing to wear them all day and teach the principle the quote addresses to anyone who asks about it. This puts students in the teaching role and takes their learning outside the classroom. Ask them to report back to you about what happened and what they learned from it.

■ Become as big as the classroom you are teaching in. In a large classroom, when you can project your voice, make bold gestures and movements, and fill the room with your presence, you increase contact with the minds of your students.

■ Keep your energy in front of you, not behind you. Your mind should be reaching out to touch the minds of your students.

■ Seek and make contact. Reach into the space between you and your students with your thoughts, voice, and movements. Work there to develop relationships and to encourage their involvement. In a large classroom, use a lapel microphone so you can move around the room easily, using the isles to reach all the students. Keep returning to the front of the room, so students in the front rows are included.

■ Success is partly measured by the participation of students in the back rows. Engage them in discussions of issues before and during class. Call on them to volunteer or participate in other ways during exercises. By reaching into the back rows, the expectation of participation is established for everyone.

■ Be spontaneous. Be ready to create from anything that is said and done. Use everything as an opportunity to learn and teach, including conflicts that arise between students.

■ Ask questions with conscious intention. Questions stimulate students to think. Use them with that idea in mind.

■ Ask students for questions while a session is underway. It helps to understand what is on their minds at that moment and to build from their questions to new ideas.

■ Use silence. Give students time to reflect on an idea or question. Avoid rushing on to the next point. Silence can also add a pause for dramatic effect, so an important idea is given special emphasis.

■ Keep your eye on the clock with the intention of creating a strong finish. Make your concluding comment captivating. The goal is to have such a strong connection with your students in the final minutes that they will not stir until after your last comment. They should be thinking about the issues when they leave.

- Challenge your students to do their best work. Have those who accept the challenge raise their hands. This anchors their commitment. Ask them to tell you how the quality of their work improved by accepting the challenge.

- Learn from student coaching. Listen to what students say about what is not working in the class. If you agree with their assessment, make the change promptly. Let the whole class know about the feedback and what you have changed, so they understand that suggestions will be seriously considered.

My large class teaching experience taught me that creativity is always possible, even in the face of limiting and challenging circumstances. I learned that, when we invite students into a dynamic learning process, they jump at the chance to be involved. When they are committed, they are more motivated to learn, to take risks, and to work hard.

Creative Spirit:
"Teach complexity today.
Take different sides of an issue."

Individual Process (30 minutes): On a journal page, identify a few topics you might cover if you were teaching a class of 500 students. Select the topic that most interests you. Write it at the top of large piece of drawing paper so you have plenty of room for design work.

With your eyes closed, imagine how a large lecture hall might look with you in the front and 500 students in their seats. Sense the excitement and challenge of teaching such a huge class. Imagine the fears you will need to manage and the personal resources you will draw on to take risks. Feel close contact with your students. See yourself effectively guiding them through an experiential exercise to a strong finish.

Having imagined yourself teaching a large class effectively, use your drawing paper to design what you would do to achieve that success in reality.

Start by identifying the topic and your specific goals for one class session. What will you want your students to learn? Be specific.

With those objectives in mind, note ideas for an opening that will capture the attention and interest of your students. Select your best idea.

Drawing on your creativity, design an innovative exercise that will lead students deeply into the issue and insure their participation. How will you involve them to achieve your objectives for the session?

When you have finished designing the session, note ideas for an effective closing. Select one that has the greatest potential for engaging the thinking of your students at the end, so they leave the classroom reflecting on the ideas.

With your session planned, close your eyes and go back into the classroom in your imagination. This time, see yourself successfully teaching what you just created.

If you are working with a partner or group, share your designs for teaching the large course, adding how you would integrate the creative ideas you developed into your existing classes.

Teaching large classes interactively is not for everyone. It takes extroverted communication skills, a willingness to take risks, and the capacity to be spontaneous. This kind of teaching drains a teacher's energy faster than normal sized classes because, to be effective, you have to become as big as the room you teach in. If it is a very large classroom, it will take a lot of energy to be that big.

There are disappointments and difficult situations to handle. The larger the class size, the more students are likely to feel anonymous, so they assume that they can walk out when they feel like it. Sometimes they have pressing engagements, such as a doctor's appointment. Do not assume that everyone leaving the classroom is unhappy. As noted earlier, this is the negative story telling that automatically begins for teachers the moment a student begins walking out. "I must be boring" or "Students don't care" are typical stories that upset us and undermine our efforts. If we can stop the stories and just state the fact–"a student is leaving and I don't know why"–we have a better chance of maintaining our ego size, balance, and effectiveness. Stating a Recovery Claim as a student leaves the room, such as "I'm good enough," is also helpful. Decide how you will respond to students walking out, because its impact on your confidence will be automatic, immediate, and damaging unless you counteract it with a positive strategy.

Challenging conflicts also arise when teaching a large class interactively, especially when it deals with social issues that people feel strongly about. I told students the first day of the semester that a large class reflects a broader range of the social divisions in society. Therefore, I expected conflicts to arise between them. "Every conflict will become a learning opportunity," I told them.

When those conflicts occurred, I reminded students about what I had said at the outset, then I asked what they were learning about society from the conflict they were having with each other. My biggest challenge occurred when a heated argument about race started to get out of control. For a time, I thought there might be violence. Students were up out of their seats, screaming back and forth at each other with threatening words. I felt temporarily helpless until I remembered, "Every conflict is a learning opportunity."

Maintaining an appearance of calm, I said: "Feelings are running very hot and deep about this issue, so something important is happening. How does your conflict with each other reflect how race is experienced by different groups in our society? What is the price society pays for that racism and the anger and hatred it produces?" These questions turned the minds of students away from their personal feelings to the social problem of race.

By the end of the session, students were focused on the broader issues and the strong emotional currents had subsided. From that situation, I learned that conflict can be turned into a good learning experience if we ask questions that guide the minds of students onto constructive pathways. Even strong emotions can be teachers if good questions arise from them.

Large classes are probably the most challenging of all teaching experiences, but there is no reason why they cannot be taught creatively, even when teaching 500 students. Those who take on the challenge of interactive teaching in these large classes receive the gratification of making education for large numbers of students more exciting, important, and meaningful.

Creative Spirit:
"Taking a risk is your willingness to discover what you haven't yet realized you can do."

When we take the risk of teaching a large class, the way opens to some of the most powerful moments in teaching.

- Seeing many minds fully concentrated on an issue or moment of learning.

- Listening to a student share a personal story that moves others to tears and understanding.

- Hearing the spontaneous laughter of so many students.

- Being in silence together, waiting expectantly for the next idea.

- Witnessing a moment of illumination when students achieve an insight together.

■ Being challenged by moments of intense conflict that become opportunities to learn.

At the end, knowing that
you respected and cared about each other,
you learned together and
education became vital and important,
you were changed by what happened, and
you will never forget it.

Creative Side Trip

Motivate students by encouraging them to teach others

Sticky name tags are a teaching resource. Write a few quotes on sticky tags that address an important issue of the class. They can be statements you create or quotes from others. Before class, ask a few students if they will wear one for the day and teach anyone who asks about it. For example, if you are teaching literature, you might take a quote from a book you are covering. If your subject is one of the sciences, it could be an important equation.

Think of a topic you will teach. Write statements in the boxes that you could use on sticky tags to encourage your students to teach others about the topic.

Chapter 23

Teaching Wisdom

*H*omelessness was a key topic in the large class I taught. I had designed an exercise that invited student volunteers to the front of the lecture hall to explore the problem from the perspective of people in different social roles. I had chosen six roles, from police officer to mother. Among them was the role of a homeless person. When the six student volunteers were in the front of the room preparing to speak, an insight came to me in the form of a question. "Shouldn't the perspective of a wise person be here?" Curious to discover what a wise person would say about homelessness, I asked if someone would play that role. A young woman far in the back of the room raised her hand and joined the others up front. She looked to be about twenty.

The students developed interesting insights about homelessness from the vantage point of their various roles. The police officer saw the issue in terms of social order, emphasizing the problems homeless people create on the streets and the pressures they put on the criminal justice system. The mother talked about how homeless people are someone's children who need to be supported for a better life. The homeless person gave a moving plea for understanding by explaining how someone becomes homeless because of economic and political changes that are beyond the control of individuals and families.

When the last of the six perspectives had been offered, I

turned to the young woman who was waiting to play the wise person. "What wisdom do you have for us about homelessness?" Without pausing to think, she began to speak. She opened her remarks by describing a healthy society as one that is balanced, where extremes of all kinds are avoided. She analyzed homelessness as a symptom of social illness and a sign that American society had fallen out of balance. She noted other examples of imbalance, such as low wages that undermine the quality of life, enormous military budgets, increasing violence on our streets, racism, and inner cities falling into decay. By describing homelessness as a symptom of a society out of balance, she gave the problem significance beyond the plight of homeless people. Her wisdom revealed the bigger picture in ways I could not have anticipated.

As she spoke, I watched the students in the massive lecture hall leaning forward in their chairs struggling to hear her every word. The room was completely quiet. With her last word, loud applause erupted. Students knew that they had heard wisdom in the words of this young woman. From then on, wisdom was cultivated when we addressed other important social issues. It provided an understanding of balance and the bigger picture.

Creative Spirit:
"When you ask your mind to be wise,
it will look for a way."

Once the importance of wisdom is fully recognized in

teaching, it can be applied broadly. What is the wise course for resolving the conflicts of gender, race, or nationalism? What is a wise way to live? A wise way to treat each other? A wise way to learn or teach? What if educational institutions were guided as much by wisdom as by rules?

Creative Spirit:
"Be wise the next time you teach."

Individual Process (10 minutes): Write "What is wisdom?" in the center of a journal page. Note your responses on the page. Afterwards, circle what you regard as wisdom's key features.

Using those features, write a short poem or paragraph about wisdom.

If you are working with a partner or group, read your work to each other. Discuss your perspectives of wisdom.

Individual Process (20 minutes): Now that you have ideas about the nature of wisdom, divide a journal page in half. In each part, note an issue where wisdom might make a difference to you. It could be related to teaching or some other aspect of your life.

Take your first issue. Close your eyes and ask yourself the simple question: "What is the wise course to take concerning this issue?" Let answers arise from the wise part of your mind. Record them.

How will you approach the issue now?

Take your second issue and repeat the process.

Contemplation: With your eyes closed, consider what you learned by using your wisdom.

If you are working with a partner or group, share your wisdom.

Many people feel others are wise but they are reluctant to admit that they are. This is a curious idea, since, as soon as we ask "What is the wise course?", the mind begins seeking an answer. The young woman in my large class became wise about homelessness because she was asked to be wise. The wisdom was already in her. The question just helped her retrieve it. When this natural tendency toward wisdom is consciously cultivated, the issues of balance and unity are brought to bear on any issue.

Creative Spirit:
"Pretend to be wise and you will discover what you have always had."

Individual Process (20 minutes): In your journal, note a topic you will teach where wisdom could make a significant difference in understanding.

Using your creativity, design an exercise that draws upon

the wisdom of your students to reveal the broader and deeper dimensions of the issue.

- How will you introduce the issue of wisdom?
- How will you help students gain access to their wisdom?
- How will they bring their wisdom to bear on the topic?

If you are working with a partner or group, share the exercise that you designed. Discuss other topics where wisdom could broaden and deepen understanding.

When you focus on wisdom, your teaching becomes sensitive to the issues of balance and unity.

How will you use wisdom in your teaching now?

How will you help your students discover and cultivate their wisdom?

Chapter 24

Looking Back

*B*y becoming more innovative teachers, we help to elevate the spirit of education. Instead of teaching being just a job, we make it into a more interesting adventure. Though our efforts, we create novel ways of engaging the minds of students so they expand their potential to learn. By cultivating the feeling of a learning community in our classrooms, we nurture mutual respect and appreciation. Knowing that our way of teaching is having an impact on the lives of our students, we feel more fulfilled as teachers. When we look back over our careers, it will be the good times, not the difficulties, that we will remember. Then, we will realize how lucky we have been to be teachers.

Looking back, recall what you accomplished through your work in *Awakening Minds*.

■ How has creativity become a more crucial part of your identity and teaching?

■ What new abilities did you cultivate and put into practice?

■ How has teaching become more interesting and fulfilling for you?

■ In what ways has your effectiveness as a teacher increased?

Take a few minutes to reflect on these questions. If you are working with a partner or group, go through the questions together, sharing your responses.

Individual Process (10 minutes): Knowing that what you accomplished as a creative teacher will continue to develop, imagine writing a book about teaching at the end of your career based on your experience.

Invent a title that captures the essence of your teaching.

Write a short poem to close the book that expresses your accomplishments as a teacher.

If you are working with a partner or group, share your book titles and poems. Discuss what you will do to continue nurturing your development as innovators.

A Personal Reflection

Over many years, the challenges and risks of expanding my creativity as a teacher have added meaning, adventure, and fulfillment to my life. I have witnessed many successes and learned not to repeat my failures. I experienced moments of happiness when my students' eyes brightened with insight and when I saw them growing in ability and understanding. Yet, there were also days when I wanted to quit teaching because they showed no interest in learning. I wrote the following haiku during one of those low moments.

What is the use of
teaching the song when so few
have the heart to sing?

Creative Spirit:
"Down? Don't give up! Forgive your students for
being tired, not talking, or failing to do their homework.
Forgive yourself for not being able to motivate them."

Although I have experienced despair at times, it will not be what I remember. Instead, I will recall hundreds of wonderful students who were willing to take risks in order to learn and change, who shared their ideas with courage, who worked hard for understanding, and who reached out to others with compassion. I will never forget the appreciation I felt for them at the end of each semester for what they had accomplished in understanding and personal growth. I will remember the appreciation they expressed toward me for what I had given them.

If I wrote a book at the end of my teaching career, I would call it "The Learning Garden: We Cultivated Understanding And Change Together." The following haiku would appear at the end.

Enchanting students.
Minds deeply cultivated.
Blossoms opening.

Creative Spirit:
"Express appreciation.
Thank your students for the gifts
they have given you—a laugh, contribution,
learning experience, or a feeling of fulfillment."

Bibliography

Hirshberg, Jerry. *The Creative Priority: Driving Innovative Business in the Real World.* New York, NY: Harper Collins Publishers, 1998.

Intrator, Sam M. *Stories of The Courage to Teach: Honoring The Teacher's Heart.* San Francisco: Jossey-Bass, 2002.

Keirsey, David. *Please Understand Me II: Temperament, Character, Intelligence.* Del Mar, CA: Prometheus Nemesis Book Company, 1998.

Kessler, Rachael. *The Soul of Education: Helping Students Find Connection, Compassion, and Character at School.* Alexandria, VA: Association for Supervision and Curriculum Development, 2000.

McKeachie, Wilbert J. *Teaching Tips: A Guide Book for the Beginning College Teacher.* Lexington, MA: D.C. Heath and Company, 1986.

McKeachie, Wilbert J. and Graham Gibbs, *McKeachie's Teaching Tips: Strategies, Research, and Theory for College and University Teachers.* Boston: Houghton Mifflin Co., 1999.

Palmer, Parker J. *The Courage To Teach: Exploring The Inner Landscape of a Teacher's Life.* San Francisco: Jossey-Bass Publishers, 1998.

Palmer, Parker J. *To Know As We Are Known: Education as a Spiritual Journey.* San Francisco, CA: Harper Collins Publishers, 1983, 1993.

Peavey, Fran. *By Life's Grace: Musings on the Essence of Social*

Change. Philadelphia, PA: New Society Publishers, 1994.

Sandler, Bernice Resnick. *Women Faculty at Work in the Classroom, or Why It Still Hurts to be a Woman in Labor* (1993). Copies of this useful book can be obtained from: HERS, Mid-America, University of Denver, MRTB 402, 2199 South University Blvd., Denver, CO 80208. Phone: (303) 871-6866; Fax: (303) 871-6866, or email [bmetzer@du.edu]. This work can also be found at her website: [www.bernicesandler.com]. Bernice Resnick Sandler is a Senior Scholar at the Women's Research and Education Institute, Washington, D. C.

Sandler, Bernice Resnick, Lisa A. Silverberg, and Roberta M. Hall, *The Chilly Classroom Climate: A Guide to Improve the Education of Women.* Copies of this book can be obtained from: HERS, Mid-America, University of Denver, MRTB 402, 2199 South University Blvd., Denver, CO 80208. Phone: (303) 871-6866; Fax: (303) 871-6866, or email [bmetzer@du.edu].

Tompkins, Jane. *A Life in School: What the Teacher Learned.* Reading, MA: Perseus Books, 1996.

"I Have A Dream" Foundation

The "I Have a Dream" Foundation helps students in low-income areas across the country work toward and realize the goal of a college education. Since its inception, it has garnered the support and personal commitment of thousands of volunteers and overseen the creation of 170 Projects in 64 cities across the country. These Projects currently serve over 13,000 Dreamers.

The "I Have a Dream" Foundation is a long-term and year-round program that works with the same group of children from their elementary schools years through high school and beyond.

It is flexible and can be tailored to suit the particular needs of its Dreamers and resources of its community. It has a "ripple effect," mobilizing untapped local resources and pulling them into Dreamers' communities, thus having an impact far beyond the Dreamers and their families.

The Program is personal. Dreamers benefit from the individual attention of a wide range of professionals and volunteers. It is also democratic. Every child in the selected group is given an equal opportunity to set and achieve attainable personal goals.

The "I Have a Dream" Program ensures success individually. The threshold goal is that all Dreamers graduate from high school and have the option to attend college or other post-secondary education and/or to obtain rewarding employment.

Beginning no later than fourth grade, Projects adopt whole grade levels of students from public elementary schools or entire age groups from public housing developments. Throughout their school years, Dreamers are provided with a comprehensive program of tutoring, mentoring, and enrichment activities. To learn more about the excellent work of "I Have a Dream" Foundation, explore its website: [www.ihad.org].

About the Author

Jim Downton has been teaching for over thirty-five years. Currently, he is a Professor of Sociology at the University of Colorado, Boulder. He teaches undergraduate courses in human development and creativity and frequently offers workshops on creative teaching for graduate students and faculty. His commitment to innovative teaching has earned him the University's two teaching excellence awards. He is also involved in the International and National Voluntary Service Training Program (INVST) at the University of Colorado, an innovative leadership training program for upper division students that emphasizes civic responsibility and community service. To learn more about INVST, visit its website: [www.colorado.edu/ArtsSciences/INVST].

In the community, Jim offers workshops on human development and creativity. In addition, he enjoys painting and sculpture. His life revolves around the issues of wholeness and creativity, which are ways of cultivating inner peace, happiness, and an easier way of living.

Printed in the United Kingdom
by Lightning Source UK Ltd.
106157UKS00001BA/5